Praise for Vision Walk
And Brandt Morgan

"*Vision Walk* opens our eyes—and more importantly our hearts—to what should be obvious common sense. This book is filled with wisdom, love, and truth."

—*Steven E*, *Creator of the*
Wake Up, Live the Life You Love *book series*
Long Beach, California

"Here is a tool that *anyone* can use at any time. If you want to learn how to get out of your head and into your heart, this book will teach you how to do it."

—*Dr. Sheri A. Rosenthal*, *Author of* The Complete Idiot's
Guide to Toltec Wisdom
Gulfport, Florida

"I feel fortunate to be among those who have touched Brandt's path. May every reader feel the blessing of his heart's knowing."

—*Jamie Sams*, *Co-author,* Medicine Cards
Santa Fe, New Mexico

"*Vision Walk* is a graceful and timely bridge between the old ways and the new. A true walk in beauty."

—*Jose H. Lucero*, *Member,*
Traditional Circle of Indian Elders and Youth
Santa Clara Pueblo, New Mexico

"Through the years, Brandt has been like a rock—truly an inspiration to many of us. Now, through *Vision Walk*, he continues to bring healing and inspiration to countless others."

—*Tom Brown, Jr.*, *Wilderness Survival Expert and*
Author of The Tracker
Fort Myers, Florida

"This is such a powerful tool. I wish more young people knew about it."
> —*Lena Samsonenko*, Natural Resources Student,
> Cornell University
> Ithaca, New York

"Brandt led me into my own heart, where I had never dared to venture before."
> —*Annick Hollender*, Chiropractor,
> Montreal, Canada

"The Vision Walk can help you experience joy, truth, and light amidst the commotion of everyday doings."
> —*Laurence Ray Simpson*, Boeing 747 Commercial Airline Pilot,
> Park City, Utah

"I can't thank Brandt and the Vision Walk enough for guiding me to be happily married to the man of my dreams."
> —*Meghan McChesney Gilroy*
> Personal Growth Seminar Leader
> Marblehead, Massachusetts

"Brandt teaches real things that really work…How easy it is to find answers if only we dare to ask."
> —*Olivier Clerc*, Writer/Editor,
> Burgundy, France

"I sometimes doubt the Vision Walk will work, but the answers always come anyway. It's just magic!"
> —*Gabrielle Addor*
> Lausanne, Switzerland

"Brandt unravels the mystery of life with his simple yet profound practice of the Vision Walk. . . . In this remarkable book you will find keys to the secret that awakens your senses and captures your hidden dreams."
> —*Pamela Harper*, Clinical Hypnotherapist
> and Certified Addiction Counselor,
> San Clemente, California

"... an amazing tool. The more I work with it, the more I trust myself."

—*Sharon Lynn Tierney*, *Retired Paramedic,*
Nevada City, California

"If you feel unhappy, broken hearted, burned out, shut down, full of longing, or you just wonder if it's possible to be free or happy in this world, Brandt's energy will take you on a walk toward freedom—a walk down a path with heart."

—*Charlene Adkins M.D.*, *Emergency Physician,*
Columbia, Missouri

"Brandt gave me back my power and filled my life with love and light. His teaching is the most magical thing I have ever experienced."

—*Monica Navarrete Mastache*, *Spiritual Psychotherapist,*
Acapulco, Mexico

"Brandt's teaching planted in me a small flame of light that is now growing into a fire of love. My only wish is to share this beautiful gift with the world."

—*Natalie Ulrich*, *Swiss Mission to the United Nations,*
New York, New York

"How lucky that there are teachers like Brandt who can lead us into a deeper, more authentic connection with nature and the divine!"

—*Shasta Cruchet*, *Art Promoter,*
Carcassonne, France

Vision Walk

Vision Walk

Asking Questions
Getting Answers
Shifting Consciousness

Brandt Morgan

Foreword by don Miguel Ruiz

PITTSBURGH

Vision Walk
Asking Questions. Getting Answers. Shifting Consciousness.

Copyright © 2006 by Brandt Morgan

ISBN-13: 978-0-9767631-4-7
ISBN-10: 0-9767631-4-1

Library of Congress Control Number: 2006927342
CIP information available upon request

First Edition, 2006

St. Lynn's Press • POB 18680 • Pittsburgh, PA 15236
412.466.0790 • www.stlynnspress.com

Cover Design – Jeff Nicoll
Book Design – Holly Wensel, NPS
Editor – Catherine Dees

Printed in the United States of America
on recycled paper ♲

In the text, the symbol for Registered Trademark is implied and
will not be used next to the references to Vision Walk™,
in order to promote ease of reading.

This title and all of St. Lynn's Press books may be
purchased for educational, business, or sales
promotional use. For information please write:
Special Markets Department, St. Lynn's Press, POB 18680,
Pittsburgh, PA 15236

10 9 8 7 6 5 4 3 2 1

This book is dedicated to my mother

Ruth Orbison Morgan

with boundless gratitude

for a lifetime of magic and love.

CONTENTS

FOREWORD
by don Miguel Ruiz
Author of *The Four Agreements*

It is a great pleasure for me to introduce Brandt Morgan and one of many magical books I know he will give to the world. When I first met Brandt in 1994, I could see that he was a complex man with many opinions. I am happy to say that he is much simpler now. Finally he gave up trying to be what he thought he should be and let himself be what he really was all along: an artist of the spirit. Now he has created a beautiful expression of his big heart—this book that you hold in your hands.

This book is simple but very powerful, and it can change your life. In it, Brandt teaches the same thing I have been teaching for many years. He shows you how to be who you really are and how to live an authentic life. In just a few pages he teaches you how to turn off your mind, enter into your heart, and use your inner guidance to find the answer to any question or problem.

The Vision Walk is a wonderful tool, and it is also very practical. When you look with your heart, you will always see the truth. And when you see the truth, you will naturally take the action that is aligned with your greatest happiness. It is just a matter of uncovering your authenticity.

Most people think becoming authentic takes a long time and is very difficult, but it is not difficult at all. Just like life, it is very simple. Your true self is always waiting for you, just beyond the noise in your mind. All you have to do is remember it and go there. With this book, you can go there in just a few minutes. In fact, I have asked Brandt to lead Vision Walks at many of my Easter gatherings, and I have seen hundreds of people find their true selves and get answers to their most important questions in less than half an hour.

Many years ago I told Brandt, "I will teach you my way, but you have to do it your way." For a long time Brandt has been teaching in his own way, and now I am glad to see him writing in his own way. Whatever he shares comes straight from the heart. As you will see, he communicates clearly and gracefully, with the wisdom of a master.

I know you will enjoy and benefit from the Vision Walk, and I hope you will use it often. It will help you to know yourself. It will help you to be happy. This book is a way to enter into the magic of creation and practice living an authentic life every day. As Brandt says, you don't need a guru to get there. It is all inside you already. So why not go there? And why not share it? After all, just being who you truly are is the greatest gift you can give to the world.

All my love,
don Miguel Angel Ruiz

PREFACE

The Vision Walk came to me one afternoon on a dusty ranch near Santa Fe, New Mexico.

It was all so simple. I was teaching a class in Toltec wisdom, much as it had been passed on to me by my own teacher, don Miguel Ruiz. Essentially, the Toltec path has to do with dropping the busy mind with all its judgments and expectations and social conditioning in order to expose the truth of who we really are. That truth is contained mainly in the heart, but after two hours I sensed that most of my students were still "up in their heads." What I was teaching seemed to be just mental concepts for them. I needed to do something different, but what?

"Send them on a vision quest," said my inner voice, reminding me of my love for the Native American path and the ritual of fasting and praying that is so important to many tribes.

"But that takes four days and nights," I protested, recalling my own experience with the ritual.

"Don't argue, just do it," the voice insisted.

"OK, do what?" I asked.

In a flash I had it all, just like downloading a computer program. I would ask my students to meditate for five minutes on a question of supreme importance, then send them out to walk in nature for 20 minutes. I would instruct them to turn off their minds and to glide over the landscape as though in a dream, constantly following their hearts and staying open to whatever might come in.

And that's what they did. When they returned from their walks, every one of those 17 students had received their answers. In fact, many of them had life-changing experiences. One student, feeling blocked and a bit depressed, was led into a ranch building, where her heart told her to sit down at a piano and play; and as she played, the notes re-awakened her dormant passion for life. A man who wanted to know how to let go of an old relationship was drawn to pick up the carcass of a cicada and realized that the life in it had already departed. As he dropped the husk back into the sand, with a smile of deep joy he also dropped his old relationship and opened up to his love for himself and all life. A third student was led to put her arms around a tree, where she felt her own heartbeat. *"Give it to me,"* the tree urged, and in a flood of tears she released an old trauma that had haunted her for years. On the surface, all of these things were very ordinary—the piano, the insect, the tree—but they became extraordinary because these people had opened themselves to everyday things as mirrors for the deeper truths within them.

For sheer drama, though, one of that day's Vision Walks topped them all: As the students were returning from their walks, the ranch cook came out to the patio with a three-gallon aluminum pot and invited us to look inside. Inside the pot was a large, hairy tarantula that had been captured in the kitchen. One by one, the students peered inside. Each had a different reaction. Some found it beautiful, others ugly. Still others recoiled in fear.

The last woman to return, however, looked into the pot, screamed in terror, and ran back into the woods. When she rejoined us, still shaking, she said in amazement, "My question was, 'Why am I always so afraid of spiders?' "

Why am I always so afraid of spiders? This might seem like a trivial question, but it was the most important thing she could have asked. In Native American mythology, Spiderwoman is the one who weaves the web of life and everything in it. We helped that woman see that the spider was *herself*—a symbol of the feminine power and creativity she had been running from all her life. In the spider she had seen her own reflection.

Was the appearance of the tarantula a coincidence? No. Nor was the beetle carcass, the piano, or the many other symbols that spoke to these Vision Walkers. There are no coincidences. All these people had drawn these symbols to themselves through the force of their own focused intent. Just as it says in the Bible: "Ask, and ye shall receive. Knock, and it shall be opened unto you." What was profoundly meaningful to one person in the group would probably not have affected another person, but in each case something specific to each person's life and question appeared in his or her path.

Since that first Vision Walk, I have facilitated countless others, both in small groups and in workshops of more than 200 people. I have even held them indoors, having people walk from room to room in search of their answers. Indoors or out, everyone has received answers, and many have been changed forever.

Today, whenever I lead a Vision Walk or read a letter describing someone's experience, I give thanks to the great mystery of life for having offered it. I knew right away that the Vision Walk was a gift, and I knew it was meant to be shared. In it I hear echoes of our collective call for freedom from the tyranny of our own minds, for another tool to help us know ourselves.

This is not a long book. I could have written more—much more—about the Vision Walk, but what would be the point? Why complicate something so simple? The same could be said about life. Why complicate it? Instead, why not just live it?

Simple, of course, doesn't necessarily mean shallow. On the surface, this book is about answering questions and solving problems, but that is only the beginning. If you allow yourself to be pulled into deeper water, the Vision Walk can take you to places *beyond* questions, *beyond* problems, beyond your wildest imaginings. It can even lead you into the ocean of your true self. All you need is the curiosity to try something new, the willingness to leave old habits behind, and the courage to be yourself.

It is my hope that when you get a glimpse of the ocean of truth behind your questions and answers—when you immerse yourself in the wisdom, love, joy, and peace inherent in this blissful state of consciousness—you will want to visit more often, or even live there all the time. And so you can.

As you begin this journey, I am tempted to say good luck, but with curiosity and courage, you won't be needing it.

HOW TO USE THIS BOOK

Chapters 1 and 2 offer brief but important background information about the Vision Walk and its roots in Native American spiritual traditions. Chapters 3 and 4 give a summary of the process and a meditation that will guide you through the Vision Walk. Chapters 5 and 6 focus on interpreting your walk. Chapter 7 looks at the subject of mastership and offers suggestions for deepening your spiritual practice. The last three chapters and the Conclusion focus on experiencing and living from your authentic self. In the Appendices you will find a variety of sample Vision Walk questions you can ask, plus letters from Vision Walkers illustrating a wide range of personal experiences, as well as journal pages where you can record your own.

Before doing your first walk, I suggest that you read or at least skim the entire book. What you learn will be well worth the time. This way, you will know where the process comes from, how it works, how others have interpreted their walks, and how to get the most out of yours.

After you begin doing the Vision Walk yourself, you can use specific chapters as references to answer questions or clarify your experiences. For example, if you have a general question about the walk, chances are it's covered in Chapter 6, Questions and Answers. If you're stumped on the meaning of your walk, you will find help in Chapter 7, Interpreting Your Walk; and in Appendix B, Letters From Vision Walkers.

Finally, while the Vision Walk can help you answer questions and solve problems, there are some things it can't do. Most important, it is not meant to take the place of professional or medical advice. If you have just been injured in a car crash, you don't need a Vision Walk, you need a doctor. If you're wondering about your legal rights, you need an attorney. You get the idea. Go wherever you can get the most reliable information. Use your common sense. The Vision Walk is for accessing inner wisdom. With inner wisdom and common sense, you've got all your bases covered.

What's It All About?

As Henry David Thoreau wrote nearly a century and a half ago, most people lead lives of quiet desperation. Our lives are so busy. We rush to and fro in cars and planes, chatter on cell phones, clack out emails, scarf down snacks, and schedule appointments. Even our leisure time is carefully calculated and sandwiched into our busy days. Sometimes it seems as if all the things that were meant to make life easier have only complicated it, cutting us off from our source of wisdom and inspiration. It's true: So many of us go from birth to death hardly knowing who we are or why we are here.

Who we are and why we're here is far grander and more exciting than most of us can imagine. Over the course of our lives, we've been conditioned to believe we are small and insignificant; that we don't deserve success and abundance; that we can't realize our most cherished dreams; that fear and anxiety are normal; and that we are unworthy of love and joy.

The truth is that beneath the masks we wear and the roles we play to protect ourselves, our true self is shining like a bright sun. It is always there. It never goes out. It is an endless source of joy and creativity. In fact, it is life itself. *We* are life itself. Every one of us, without exception, is intimately connected to the Creator and to all living things. Through this connection, anything is possible—including the innate ability to answer almost any question imaginable.

Questions, Questions

Life is full of questions. Hardly a day goes by when we aren't faced with nagging problems and important choices. Our questions range from the profound to the mundane: "Why am I here? What do I really want? What is the highest expression of my talents and abilities? Should I stay in this relationship? How can I make more money? How can I improve my health? Can I trust my stockbroker? Shall I go to the party this weekend? What shall we do for dinner tonight? Shall I buy an SUV or an economy car? And, oh yeah, where did I leave the car keys?"

We look almost anywhere for the answers. We ask

friends for advice on our love lives. We consult the *I Ching* about whether we should take a vacation to Bali or the Bahamas. We ask astrologers to tell us how to align ourselves with the stars. We ask Tarot readers to tell us whether we're on track to fulfill our life's purpose. And every day we're bombarded by advertisements telling us who we are, who we *should* be, and what we need in order to be happy and fulfilled, prettier, or more popular.

Useful and entertaining as these things are, most of the time they aren't necessary. Why? *Because you already have the answers.* They're inside you. No confidant, counselor, or divination system can tell you much more than you already know. You don't need a friend to tell you how to live your life. You don't need a sage or a psychology book to tell you how to find true love. And you don't need to listen to all those advertisements that tell you what products to buy—not toothpaste or beer or baloney. In most cases, all you need to do is consult yourself—or perhaps I should say the self *beyond* the self. I like to call this self the real you.

The Real You

I want to clarify what I mean by *the real you* because it is the most important term you will encounter in this book. From time to time I also call it your *true self* or your *authentic self*. Sometimes I even refer to it as *awareness* or *life*. I don't capitalize any of these terms because we tend to think capitalized words represent something separate, special, and unattainable—for example, the term *God* as it is used in most religions. Ordinary lowercase terms like *awareness* and *life* are still wonderful and mysterious, but they don't seem like such a big deal. In the end, though, all these terms—including *God*—are little more than signposts pointing to a reality that is beyond words.

Most of us think we are our bodies, minds, emotions, and personalities. The real you has nothing to do with who you think you are. It has nothing to do with thinking at all. The real you exists only in the *absence* of thought.

The real you permeates your mind and body, but it is neither. It contains all creation, but it is no thing. The real you is vast, formless, and forever. Yet at the same time, it is not void or empty; it is full of light, love, and joy. It is a great, living mystery. It is the very source of life and all creation. The real you is the no-thing that gives rise to everything. It is pure awareness beyond form.

The real you sees, hears, and feels through your body, but it is not your body. Your body is contained within it, and so is everything else. To the real you, your body is mainly a tool of perception, like a pair of 3-D glasses you put on at the movies. Through our human senses, forms appear separate from each other, but we are not separate from anything. At the level of the real you, you are one with all creation. In fact, the entire universe and everything in it is only one thing—one grand, omniscient being that has magically and magnificently projected itself into trillions of different forms.

Your personal body-mind is one of those forms. You are a human, but you are also the universe. Using a common metaphor, you are a drop of water, but you are also the ocean.

For many years I thought I knew what that meant—intellectually, at least—until one night, when I had an unusual dream; and then I finally got it. In this dream I was sitting in a boat no bigger than a bathtub, being tossed about in an ocean storm with mountainous waves swelling and foaming all around me. I thought to myself, *Boy, it's lucky I have this boat, or I'd really be in a fix!*

In that moment the boat disappeared, and I was left treading water, a speck of life adrift in a hostile sea. *I'm going to be crushed by the next wave and drown!* But then I felt something strange. It was as though the water around me suddenly became loving arms buoying me up. With an answering rush of love I welcomed their embrace. *I am not separate from the ocean!* I realized. *It is a part of me!*

Just as this thought crossed my mind, a killer whale exploded upwards and arced gracefully back into the water, trailing a magnificent rainbow of spray. *Oh joy!* I thought, *the whale is a part of me, too!*

Yet no sooner did the whale disappear than I began thinking, *Where did he go? Maybe he's coming to eat me!* Then the whale leaped from the water again, and I knew he was part of me and we were both part of the ocean. When the whale disappeared from my sight once more, I became the drop again, separate and fearful. This rapid and radical shift in consciousness went on for quite a while, back and forth, before I woke up and realized what the dream was trying to tell me: "You see, you are the ocean *and* the drop. But most of the time you think you're just the drop. That's why you live in fear. The trick is to wake up and be the drop while *knowing* you're the ocean. Believing is not enough. Faith is not enough. You have to *know* it. *Then* the truth will set you free."

That is the magic of the real you. The ocean of consciousness is waiting for us to wake up. When we do, it comes alive inside and all around us, and it stretches to the depths and ends of the universe. There is a part of the real you in every galaxy, every teacup, every blade of grass. The real you is always and everywhere, one with the one and only One. At the deepest level, we are life experiencing itself through human thought and emotion, life dancing and playing and creating dramas and crying and laughing and smiling at the myriad faces of itself, life delighting in its own reflection.

Your personal ego self wants you to think you are separate from the Creator so that it can continue to control your life. Your ego wants you to think you are your mind with its heady collection of thoughts, beliefs, regrets, fears, and dramas so that it can continue suffering and creating problems. In comparison to the real you, the mind is hardly more than an inflatable toy or a stuffed rag doll.

Just imagine for a moment that your perception suddenly turned inside-out; that instead of seeing the universe through the eyes of a human, you were now seeing a human through the eyes of the universe. Imagine that you are the universal life force itself. Imagine that you are pure, vibrant awareness; that with your love you created all things; that you have seen galaxies come and go; and that over the eons your greatest joy has been to express and experience yourself through all your varied creations. This is not ego; this is just a different point of view, a shift in consciousness. Far from being a selfish point of view, this is the most selfless viewpoint imaginable—no self at all!

Now imagine you are formless, but that for the fun of it you decided to project yourself into all the forms you created. Imagine you are inside the body of a human being (and everything else) but that you see it more as a costume to slip into each day so that you can interact with other humans—all of whom are also you in disguise. Imagine you are life itself watching a movie that you wrote, directed, and are starring in yourself.

Do you notice what happens when you do this? How can you get worried or anxious when you know it's just a movie? How can you take anything personally if you know you're not really a separate person? How can you be afraid of dying when you know you're immortal? How can you get worked up about life when you *are* life? (The Real You Meditation in Chapter 10 goes deeper into this great mystery.)

Ultimately, the real you is beyond words. Call it intuition. Call it universal consciousness. Call it life. Call it awareness. Call it God or Being or your Buddha nature. Whatever you call it, this infinitely wise presence waits patiently and peacefully in the recesses of your heart, trying to get through to you. It has always been there, always will be there, shining like a beacon beneath all the social masks, all the musts and shoulds, all the have-to's and not-good-enoughs that have kept you from knowing it.

The real you is the part of you that speaks in your dreams, wakes you up in the middle of the night with a new idea, nudges you gently in a new direction, and sometimes screams at you when you're about to do something stupid. It is a fountain of truth, the source of anything you could ever want to know. All the wisdom of past, present, and future is contained in the real you. But ah—how to get in touch with it? Now, *that* is the question!

2

Ancient Origins

The Vision Walk is a way to get the ego self out of the way, get the mind out of the way, and re-connect with the real you. By now you are probably eager to do exactly that. If this is the case, turn to Chapter 3, Let's Take a Walk, and come back to this one later. But be sure to come back soon, because this chapter explains where the Vision Walk comes from and how it works. In the long run, it will give you a much more solid foundation for your walks.

In most native cultures around the world, there is an ancient tradition called the *vision quest*. This is a very special time when a young person goes into the wilderness to commune with nature and ask for a dream or vision that will reveal his or her gifts and place in the tribe. Usually it is done around the time of puberty, but it can take place at any time.

In many cultures, the quester spends four days and nights inside a 10-foot circle meditating, dancing, and praying to the Great Mystery. Distractions are kept to a minimum. Often with little more than a blanket, the young person fasts from food and sometimes even water in order to open more fully to the spirit world. As body and mind begin to lose energy and quiet down, the deeper messages begin to come. Sometimes they come in the form of grand dreams or visions, but more often they come in much more subtle ways. A bird lights on a branch and scolds the quester to look deeper. A tiny seedling reminds the quester of the innocence of children and the preciousness of new life. A rotting stump speaks of death and rebirth. A passing deer awakens the spirit of forgiveness. In the stillness and clarity of nature, everything becomes a mirror in which the quester can receive answers to his questions and see himself more clearly.

Vision quests are not common in modern society, but they are becoming more popular all the time. Led by teachers whose own lives have been touched by it, increasing numbers of people are using the quest as a means of discovering their true selves and finding new direction and inspiration.

I did my first vision quest in the Pine Barrens of New Jersey in 1983, under the direction of my teacher,

Tom Brown, Jr., who had been taught the Native American arts of survival and nature awareness by an old Lipan Apache scout named Stalking Wolf.

Generally, vision quests are deeply personal and rarely spoken of, except with one's teachers. But I would like to share with you my own experience of that first quest—partly because it was a long time ago, and partly because it shows what can happen when you open yourself up to a shift in consciousness.

I'll never forget the night before it began. Twenty-eight of us were huddled inside a makeshift shelter among the pines, trying to stay warm and dry in the midst of a major rainstorm. Outside, lightning and thunder were ripping the sky apart. As Tom spoke, I could feel the fabric of my life coming apart at the seams.

"Whatever fear you're feeling right now is not the fear of wild dogs or sickness or storms or the dark," Tom said. "It's the fear of really knowing yourself."

Truer words were never spoken, I thought. I wondered whether I would be able to face that fear, and what I might find if I did.

"It's a shocker to a lot of people when they find out who they are," Tom went on. "It can cause a real disruption in their lives. That's because most people live a life they don't really own."

Did I live my own life, I wondered, or was it

someone else's? I could feel my social conditioning squirming inside: my mother's perfectionism, my father's preoccupation with money and success, the fragile self-image that, in spite of my outward success—money, women, friends, and creative work in the publishing business—always seemed to be seeking more approval. Would this vision quest bring me inner peace? Would it show me who I really was? And if it did, what would it ask me to do?

As for the spiritual side of the quest, even though I had already co-authored two of the first four books in Tom's wilderness survival series and was familiar with his philosophy of oneness with all things, I had little idea how deep that philosophy went. I told myself I was doing this quest because Tom had asked me to do it and so I could write with more authority. I was about to discover that I was seriously deluding myself.

Wind and rain kept battering the shelter as Tom spoke. "After a day or two in the circle, you people will get so exhausted and tired and frustrated that finally your mind will just shut down. The logical, thinking mind—the mind that we have trained since kindergarten—goes to sleep. Then something very wonderful happens. A pair of heavy steel gates flies open and you walk to the other side. When this happens, the deep inner self begins to speak to you. Your thought is no longer your thought; it is who you are. It is the whole realm of Creation and the very voice of the Creator. The Great Spirit uses nature to communicate with you. And since you are a part of all things, any part of nature will be used to contact your "self."

"Isn't it crazy?" Tom asked. "It's almost like two different people. In fact, it is! But that self does not speak to you in words. The true self does not have any language as we know it. It's a spirit language, a language of dreams and symbols."

I had already had a taste of that symbolic language the previous day when I had staked out my quest area and become entranced watching an inchworm. This worm, like no other I had seen, was hanging halfway between a tree branch and the earth, completely tangled up in its lifeline. Through some combination of indecision and wrong moves, the silken thread on which thousands of other worms were dropping down to begin their earthly adventures had for this worm become a confining prison. Now, unable to go up or down, the little thing was expending all of its energies getting nowhere. *How like a human,* I thought. *How like me!*

Tom spoke of logistics and what to expect during the quest. He said that we would be allowed to leave our circles only to relieve ourselves and to pick up a fresh gallon of water that would be left at the edge of the road each night. I had never gone four days without food, but I knew it was an essential part of the process. Over the four-day period, he explained, we would probably experience a succession of emotions ranging from boredom and frustration to elation and deep peace. He said we would seek out anything to entertain ourselves and feed our logical minds: birds, squirrels, inchworms, the varying shapes of leaves, even the flatness of dust. He warned that we would probably go over and over our personal ruts and routines, relive our successes and failures, and evaluate jobs and relationships trying to find meaning and continuity in our lives. He also said that we would probably cuss him up and down when the going got tough and be tempted again and again to call it quits.

"You are going to go through hell, people, but you are also going to pass through the gates of consciousness. You are going to enter into a world that very few people these days either feel, see, or experience in any way—the world of the spirit, the world of something greater than self.

"And I'll tell you something else," he added ominously. "If you're looking for a vision just for yourself, there will be no vision. You must seek a vision for all things in the sacred circle."

Tom paused, then said, "That's it. Tomorrow morning you go to your graves. I have spoken." As if on cue, the shelter lit up with a searing flash of light punctuated by a deafening clap of thunder.

The next morning before sunup, I walked barefoot down the camp road, then through thick brush to the quest area I had marked out the day before. It was an isolated, 10-foot circle surrounded by scrub oaks and pines. First I set up a tarp in the tree branches, just above my sitting and sleeping area, to protect me from the rain. Then I placed my sleeping bag and other gear completely out of sight. Finally, when everything felt just right, I knelt and prayed to the Creator to show me how to do a vision quest.

I soon got an urge to move, so I stripped to my running shorts and began dancing around the circle. Round and round I went in a shuffling, monotonous two-step. My bare feet began flattening twigs, oak leaves, and pine needles, creating a rudimentary pathway. After several hours, I began humming a low, rhythmical chant that took me into a light trance. Without knowing why, I also began focusing on the little oak bush in the center of the circle, continually singing to it and sending it love through my heart and the movements of my hands. Round and round I went, chanting and dancing, dancing and chanting, stopping occasionally to stretch, meditate, or pray beneath the shady pine tree that marked the east side of my circle.

When I tired of dancing and chanting, I did

pushups or pull-ups. When I tired of that, I watched ants and inchworms, or listened to towhees scratching among leaves, or woodpeckers rapping on tree trunks. When the sun was shining, I guzzled lots of Pine Barrens spring water from a plastic gallon container. When it rained, I sat under my tarp watching rivulets of water trickle onto the ground. When the sun came out again, I danced some more.

By the afternoon of the first day, my feet had worn a clear path into the sandy soil, a circle around a mound of dirt, with my small oak bush at its center. As I danced, I chanted and prayed, sending all my love and energy to the central mound—again, not really knowing why. I began to notice that my feet were throwing off wonderful spiral patterns in the sand. I danced most of the first night.

When the sun rose on the morning of the second day, I looked at where I had danced and was astonished at what I saw. The new light revealed a marvelous pattern in my dance ground, a spinning sandy galaxy with sweeping arms of stars reaching out into a forest universe. In the center of the spiral form, now clearly defined by the deep path encircling it, was the earth itself—the mound And growing from the very center of the earth was the little oak, no more than a foot tall. In a flash of recognition I saw what it really was: the universal Tree of Life.

In awe I knelt down and reached into the center of the sandy "galaxy" I had so lovingly created during the night. There, in the middle of the spiral field, I discovered one tiny root from the central tree that had been exposed by my dancing. The root seemed to be reaching into the stars like an eager tendril. I was especially struck by the fragility of the root. I knew that it represented something very important and precious within me, something I had never consciously known but that had the power to change my entire life. During the remainder of my dancing, whenever I came around to that little root, I stepped very carefully. To break it would have broken my heart.

I didn't fully understand the meaning of my vision that morning, or for many mornings afterward. In fact, it continues to grow in me even now. But I felt it profoundly. Months later, while reading *Black Elk Speaks*, the autobiography of the famous visionary and chief of the Oglala Sioux, I came across a prayer the old man spoke shortly before his death. Despairing that he had not fulfilled his vision but still clinging to the hope that his people and their way of life would not vanish, he said, "It may be that some small root of the sacred tree still lives. Nourish it, then, that it may leaf and bloom and fill with singing birds."

Even before I had finished my vision quest, I knew deep inside that my life was about finding my roots to the earth and nourishing the sacred tree within me. In the same way the little tendril was drawing nourishment from the space between the stars, my job was to draw nourishment from the space between thoughts, to look beyond beliefs and search in silence for the truth: the truth of what I am, the truth of what we all are, and the wonder of what we are doing here on this beautiful, blue marble spinning at the edge of its spiral galaxy in the blackness of space. More than that, I knew that my greatest joy in life would come through sharing what I discovered. For me, this book is a part of that joy.

There was more, much more, to my vision quest in the Pine Barrens, but that was the heart of it. As I continued orbiting my little "earth mound," I talked to hawks and owls, bees and butterflies. I baked in the sun and felt my roots sinking deeper into the earth. I came to see animals, plants, trees, clouds, and stars as friends and fellow travelers. They taught me a thousand ways to express my gratitude, a thousand ways to pray.

With no food, little sleep, and a growing awareness of everything around me, I sank further into the spirit world, receiving precious messages from my circle and from a place deep within me. Kneeling at the edge of the circle on the morning of the third day, I reached my hand out to touch the beautiful pattern of spirals, and a voice inside said, "Yes, this is your spiral galaxy, but more accurately it is mine. I created it, just like I created the heavens and the earth, then dropped your body down here like an inchworm from the Tree of Life. Why? To experience myself in human form, of course. To enjoy myself. To live, to laugh, to love, and ultimately to return to the ocean of all that I am. I am you. You are me. We are one and always will be."

I was staggered by these words. It was the ocean talking to the drop. This was the voice of my true self, the same divine awareness that was present in the very beginning, speaking clearly to one of its beloved creations—myself. I also knew that this same divine awareness was in everyone.

By now, all my perceptions had been turned on their head. I knew that what I normally saw as solid reality was only a symbol for the much deeper reality enshrouded within it. I saw clearly how everyone and everything is already one with the Creator without realizing it; how our spirits merge with each other and the universe; and how we continually create and recreate the heavens and the earth together.

As I lay in my sleeping bag on the last night, katydids laughed and crickets chirped in an almost deafening symphony. Satellites glided across the sky like pinpricks of light. I could hear tires roaring against the surface of the New Jersey Parkway miles off. Jets passed overhead, their blinking lights signaling other aircraft bound to and from Newark and New York. The humid smell of the salt ocean blended with the sands of ancient seas beneath my mattress of oak leaves. Gently, the world began calling me back.

On the morning of the fifth day, I stood barefoot in my circle one last time and asked if it had anything more to say.

"Remember that every day is sacred, every day a gift," it said. "You have danced your devotion to the earth, you have revealed your true path. Now commit yourself to it. Now make it real. Let your spiritual roots grow deeper. Listen to the messages that arise from the earth and all its creatures. All you do, do with reverence and love." Then the voice seemed to chuckle. "And don't forget the little things. Even sipping a cup of coffee can be an expression of your higher being!"

Finally, I gathered up my things and walked out of the Pine Barrens with a song in my heart. I had communed with the Source, and I knew my life would never be the same.

I was right. My first vision quest was the opening of a doorway that has led me ever deeper into the spirit world, ever deeper into life. No, it didn't solve all my problems or take away all my doubts and fears, but it showed me who I was. It gave me a sense of purpose and direction, a fixed star by which to navigate. It told me what to do and how to live.

Not that I haven't made mistakes or gotten side-tracked—far from it. But in retrospect, every misstep has been an important part of the journey. Even now, that first vision quest shines like a beacon, bringing me back again and again to the source of life and my reason for being here. It was the inspiration for this book and for many other things I've written or taught over the past two decades. Along with becoming a father, it was one of the most transformative experiences of my life.

It is fitting that the Vision Walk was inspired by the Native American vision quest. Ancient wisdom returns in many times and places to transmit the truth in new and unexpected forms. While there is nothing like a traditional vision quest for reaching the deeper levels of spirit and gathering the inspiration and energy for a new direction, the inescapable truth is that few of us have either the time or the willingness to undergo such a extreme ritual experience. For those who wish to explore the possibility further, I strongly recommend it. (See the "Vision" page on my website at www.brandtmorgan.com.)

The good news is that it isn't necessary to spend four days and nights inside a 10-foot circle in order to find out who you are and what you came here to do, or to answer most of the myriad other questions that come up in daily life. You don't have to be alone in a pine forest; it can happen anywhere. If you're in the right frame of mind you can receive profound, life-changing answers from a billboard or even a barstool. And that is where the Vision Walk comes in.

Though the Vision Walk is focused on answering one specific question rather than being open ended, it works just like a vision quest. The principle is exactly the same: You shut down the mind and open the heart. You soften the boundaries between you and your surroundings. But you do all this in minutes instead of hours or days. From start to finish, the Vision Walk usually takes less than half an hour. All it takes is relaxed attention, clear focus, and a little faith.

3

Let's Take A Walk

The beauty of the Vision Walk is that you can do it almost anytime or anywhere: on a weekend getaway to the beach, during a hike in the mountains, on a layover at the airport, in the comfort of your own home, even on your lunch hour or a coffee break. Here are the simple steps in the process:

1. **Get clear on your question.** Pick one question and stick with it. It can be any question—specific, open-ended, or yes-or-no, but make sure it is a question that is important to you. Keep your question as simple as possible. The shorter the better. Also pay attention to how you frame your question. Generally, if you frame your questions in the positive—for example,

"How can I succeed?" rather than "Why can't I succeed?" you will get more positive answers. For a list of questions to stimulate your mind, see Appendix A, Suggestions for Questions.

2. **Get into a deeply relaxed, meditative state.** If you already have a way that works for you, use it. If not, use the Vision Walk Meditation in Chapter 4.

3. **Meditate on your question for five minutes.** Just hold the question in your mind and energize it with your thoughts. Repeat it over and over like a mantra. Repeat it with *feeling*. Feel your question bubbling up from deep down inside. Feel it with your whole body.

4. **Release your question to the universe.** The method I use most often is to imagine I'm blowing up a brightly colored helium balloon with my question written on it, then visualize it sailing off into the sky. (Again, refer to the Vision Walk Meditation in Chapter 4.)

5. **Begin walking, following your heart.** Walk slowly, silently, as though floating in a dream. Meander from place to place without

destination, without thinking. Your heart knows exactly where to find the answer. Follow it without question and do exactly as it says.

6. **Be attentive, expecting an answer.** Don't be attached to how your answer will come. It will come to you in a way that is unique to you, in a way that reflects the truth that is already inside you. Maybe you will see it on a traffic sign. Maybe you will hear it in the call of a dove. Maybe you will feel it spontaneously arising from inside. Anything can be your answer.

7. **Recognize your answer.** Most often you will feel your answer in your whole body. You will just *know*. Sometimes it will come to you right away, and sometimes it will come to you later. If you don't know your answer after 30 minutes, refer to Chapter 5, Questions and Answers; and Chapter 6, Interpreting Your Walk. Appendix B, Letters From Vision Walkers, may also be helpful for you in analyzing the main symbols and experiences in your walk.

8. **Be grateful, take action.** Take a moment to silently thank yourself and the universe, to feel the magical connection between the personal

you and the real you. Then take action. Do what your walk tells you to do. This honors the gift and makes room for more magic. It also strengthens your connection with spirit, opening the door to even more gifts and miracles.

4

The Vision Walk Meditation

After you have done a few Vision Walks, you may not need any special aids to turn off your mind and sink into a deep state of awareness. For starters, though, I strongly recommend that you use the following Vision Walk Meditation to help you relax, frame your question, and release it. Have someone read it to you in a calm, soothing voice. Better yet, record it in your own voice and play it for yourself before your walk. (Or you can purchase the Vision Walk CD on my website for an audio version of the Vision Walk Meditation.)

If you record the meditation yourself or have it read to you by someone else, read it slowly and deliberately, calmly but with feeling, as if you were reading to a child at bedtime. Also remember to pause between sentences and when you encounter dots like this: ...

OK, let's start by taking a deep breath. . . . And relax as you let it out. . . . Now another deep breath . . . and let it out. . . . As you inhale the next breath, breathe in the light that surrounds your body. See and feel the light of your spirit as a luminous egg, shimmering silvery gold, extending about a foot beyond your physical form, protecting and soothing, bathing your body in the light of the real you.

This luminous egg is fed by the light of the sun and the spirit that moves through all things. Breathe in this light. . . . Feel it as it enters your lungs and moves into your bloodstream. Feel it as it rushes to your heart. Feel it as it's pumped into the arteries and capillaries that feed your physical body. Let it penetrate and permeate every organ, every bone, every muscle, every cell.

As you breathe in, allow yourself to be nourished by the light. As you breathe out, release any cares about the past or future, any sense of worry or concern, any darkness, any fear. Breathe in that wonderful, renewing, rejuvenating life force. . . And again, breathe out all that does not need to remain. Allow yourself to simply sink. . . down. . . down. . . down, into the ocean of your own deeper consciousness. . . . Now you are completely relaxed and in a deep state of inner peace. . . .

Now imagine that you're in a control room. This control room is filled with telephones, computer consoles, and blinking lights. There are also lots people typing, talking on the phones, and rushing to and fro delivering messages. Take a moment to observe this space. Feel the amazing energy and activity here. . . . This is the control room of your mind, and it is time to turn it off.

The main power switch is over there—on the wall next to the elevator. Walk over to the power switch. . . . Good. Now reach up with one hand, grab hold of the switch, and pull it down. Watch the power go off in the control room. The lights dim and go out. The computer screens go blank. People slump at their desks. All activity ceases. With the exception of a few blinking lights, it's dark now and the mind is completely quiet. You won't be needing the mind for this exercise, but it will still take care of your body while you are gone.

Right next to the power switch is an elevator with an open door. Go over to the elevator and step inside. Good. You are going to take the elevator down several floors. Just push the heart-shaped button on the console—the one that says "Heart Chamber". . . That's it. You're going down now. . . down into the heart chamber. . . down . . . down. . . down. Good. You are gently descending into a space where you are always connected to your true self, the real you. You are about to enter a very special room—a place of infinite peace and joy, a place of unbounded creativity and wisdom. You can already feel the energy of this wondrous space emanating from the chamber as the elevator comes to a gentle stop.

Now the elevator door opens, and you rejoice as you step slowly into your heart chamber. You feel bathed in peace and love. Allow yourself to feel the deep joy of this homecoming . . . Now walk deeper into this space of truth. Take your time. Notice what the chamber looks like. Notice how it feels. . . . Allow yourself to absorb its wonderful energy. This is the core of your being, the heart of the real you.

Take another moment to savor this room. Feel your intimate connection to the earth and all creation; to plants and animals, planets and stars. Feel your oneness with and deep love for all humanity. Notice the portals to past and future. Gaze at the magical doorways that give you access to all the wisdom of the universe.

Now look toward the middle of your heart chamber. In the very center is a plush, reclining couch, perfectly formed to fit your body. Glide over and take a closer look. Notice the color, shape, and texture of the couch. Reach out and feel its softness. Now sit back in the couch. Just sink into it and observe your chamber. Never have you felt so deeply peaceful and relaxed.

As you lie back on the couch, close your eyes and allow yourself to formulate your question. Keep it short and simple. This is the question that is most important to you, the question you most want to answer right now. You know what it is. If you've forgotten, relax and it will come to you. . . .

During the next few minutes, allow that question to become a part of you. Focus on your question and nothing else. Dwell on it. Feel it. Repeat it over and over like a mantra. Allow it to permeate your whole body. Allow it to seep into every cell. Become your question. Take two or three minutes in silence to do this. . . .

(Two or three minutes later): OK, now that your question is very clear, and now that it is contained within your entire body, begin to draw the energy of the question into your lung area. With each in-breath, see and feel the energy of your question pulling in from your extremities and compacting into your lungs. It's coming in now—from fingers and toes; from arms and legs; from head, chest, and abdomen.

The energy of your question pulls in and compacts into a ball in the center of your lungs. Notice its color and shape. Notice how it spins as it draws more energy into itself. Keep drawing it in until all the energy of your question is contained within this ball in the center of your lungs. . . .

Now all of the energy of your question is inside your lungs. Now imagine holding a deflated yellow balloon in the fingers of one hand—a flat, yellow, deflated balloon. Feel the rubbery texture in your fingers. When you're ready, lift the balloon to your lips and blow the energy of your question into it. That's right, just blow up the balloon.

The energy of your question is leaving your lungs and

filling the balloon with helium. Feel it going out, and watch the balloon expand as you blow. Three or four good breaths should do it. . . . Good. Now the balloon is fully inflated and all the energy of your question is inside. Already you can feel the balloon straining to lift into the sky. But hold onto it a minute more.

Be sure to tie a knot in the balloon before you let it go. Feel the texture of the balloon in your hands. Hear the rubbery, hollow sound of your fingers scraping against the fully inflated balloon. Next, imagine some colorful streamers attached to the balloon so it will be more visible in the air. Your balloon is straining to take off now. But before you let it go, see your question written clearly on the side in big, bold letters. . . .

Now, at last, hold your decorated balloon aloft in your fingers . . . and let it go. . . . There it goes. Look—up into the sky. Watch it sail away . . . up, up, up. It's bobbing and sailing on the wind now—up into the clouds. It's getting smaller now, smaller—rising into the clear, blue sky. . . . The writing is barely visible now. Getting smaller, smaller . . . Now the balloon becomes a dot . . . and disappears.

At last, your question has been released. It has been sent and delivered to the Source, where all questions are immediately answered. It's as easy as ask and receive. The answer to your question has already been sent. All you have to do is find it.

In a moment you're going to open your eyes and listen to your heart. If it tells you to meditate, stay and meditate. If it tells you to walk to the parking lot, walk to the parking lot. If it tells you to wander outside, wander outside. If you're inside, glide from room to room. Walk as though you were floating in a dream. Be relaxed but attentive to the things around you.

You will receive your answer in the way that is just right for you. It will be given in something you see, hear, smell, taste, or touch—maybe even something you feel or do. Don't prejudge how your answer will come. It will be very specific, and it will be clear and unmistakable. Now open your eyes and begin your walk.

Continue your Vision Walk for five to 20 minutes— no more than half an hour. When you get your answer, take a moment to savor it. Feel the magic and wonder of the process. Appreciate the wisdom of the real you, the no-self that is unbounded by space, time, or limitations. Open your heart in gratitude. Then take action on your answer and watch your life change for the better! . . .

Once you have taken your first Vision Walk, you will probably have questions. All this may be new to you. There may be things that didn't fit your expectations, or you may doubt that you got the "right" answer. Maybe you aren't sure you're doing it right.

Or maybe it was so different from your usual experiences that you're wondering how to bring it down to earth. If so, the next chapter will be helpful.

5

Questions and Answers

What follows are some of the most frequently asked questions about the Vision Walk. The answers will give you a clearer picture of how the process works and how to interpret it. For more, see Chapter 6, Interpreting Your Walk; and Appendix B, Letters From Vision Walkers.

What if I didn't get an answer?

About three out of every 100 people who do the Vision Walk say, "I didn't get an answer." I always tell them, "Yes you did; you just don't know it yet."

If you think you didn't get an answer, go back over your Vision Walk in detail. Remember the things you saw, heard, smelled, tasted, or touched. Remember the things you did, the places you went, everything about it. Look at it just like a dream. Imagine that everything in your walk is a mirror that reflects some aspect of you or your life. Then ask, "What part of me is this? What part of me is that? What does this represent? What does that represent? What are these things trying to tell me?"

During one Vision Walk, a man named Jeff asked, "Where is my abundance going to come from?" and thought he hadn't gotten an answer. I had him go back over the main elements of his walk, and nothing stood out. Then I asked, "Where did you go? What did you do?" Finally he remembered he had gone to sit in a swing in order to relax and open up. Then he remembered actually swinging and feeling like a little boy again.

Suddenly he realized, "Of course! Swings are for kids! What kids like to do is play and have fun. My abundance will come from having fun and doing what I love!"

Now, this may not have meant the same thing to someone else, but remember, this is Jeff's true self speaking to him in ways that will lead him to his answer. After getting this basic answer, Jeff could then ask more specific questions—for example, "What do I most like to do?" And after that, "How can I make a good living at it?"

How do I know the answer is true?

The Vision Walk doesn't lie. You'll know it with your whole body. If you relax and allow it to happen, the answers you get will be from the real you. Your mind may misinterpret the answer or try to talk you out of it, but the truth will be in your feelings, not in what you think. If you find yourself in an argument with yourself, second-guessing your answer or trying to figure something out, your mind has slipped back in again. Just go back to your heart, back to the original feeling, and the truth will come to you. If all else fails, do another Vision Walk with the question, "Is this answer true?" or "How do I know the answer is true?"

What if I don't like the answer?

Actually, that is a fairly common situation. Sometimes I've gotten answers I didn't like or that I tried to talk myself out of. So have some of my students. In fact, usually the reason a person "doesn't get an answer" or "can't figure it out" is because they're not ready to hear it. The mind puts up a wall to prevent it from coming through. Usually this is because there is something we don't want to admit or let go of. This is called denial, and it is simply a resistance to being the real you. That's OK; we always have free will. But when your mind overrides the deeper wisdom of your heart, the results can be painful or disappointing.

What can happen when you ignore your answer?
Here is one example: One of my students who had mixed feelings about a woman asked the question, "Should I pursue this relationship?" His walk took him to a cyclone fence topped with barbed wire, where he saw a sign that read, "NO TRESPASSING. VIOLATORS WILL BE PROSECUTED." He pursued the relationship anyway, and he suffered greatly during the breakup shortly afterwards.

Another example: On the enthusiastic recommendation of my broker, I made some investments in the stock market. Some of them were particularly risky, but my broker assured me they would pan out. Even as they rapidly gained in value, however, I had a gnawing feeling that the trend might not last. So I went on a Vision Walk to ask for advice.

On my walk I saw a California state flag billowing in a stiff breeze. The main feature on the California flag, of course, is the bear. This immediately set off an internal alarm about an impending "bear market."

Looking back, I clearly felt the truth of the answer. I knew the market was about to take a dive. However, I still *wanted* to believe that my broker was right. After all, he was the expert, wasn't he? Two days later the market took a tumble and continued falling for months.

Why don't we follow our inner voice?

For one thing, we're used to following everyone *else's* voice. For another, we're afraid to change our old habits. Just as common, the answer may seem too good to be true.

Remember, these answers are coming from the real you—the part of you that knows no bounds, no limits, no fears. Often the small self, the ego that is listening in and filtering the answer, just can't imagine your being as big or wonderful as the Vision Walk says you are. So it argues with the real you. It will use every trick in the book to keep you small and maintain control of your life. So finally you may decide to play it safe rather than taking the risk. Or you may decide to go against yourself, even though you know it will be painful.

This is fine, since it's all learning. In the end, there is no right or wrong. Just keep asking questions, getting answers, and taking action. With practice you will discover that life is much easier and happier when the real you is in the driver's seat.

What do you mean by listening with your heart?

I mean being still and mindless, open and receptive. Let me give you an example: Shari, an attractive but tough policewoman in the gang unit of the San Diego County Sheriff's Department, was dissatisfied with her work. All her life she had been taught to protect and defend. She felt there must be something more. Sitting on a park bench near the ocean, she asked the question, "What have I come here to do? What is my purpose in life?"

In less than five minutes, Shari was led toward the marble sculpture of a seal beside a children's playground. Even before she reached the statue, it "spoke" to her, saying, "You know, Shari. You know. Your purpose is to love. Remember? Just love, that's all." And she broke into tears. That moment was a major turning point in her life.

Of course, someone could have told Shari that her purpose was to love, and she might have gotten it in her mind, but she wouldn't have gotten it in her heart. When you listen with your heart, your whole body resounds like a church bell, and the truth comes rushing in.

Are there any other keys to getting answers?
Yes. Pay attention to your *feelings*. In the dining room of a magnificent home in Carlsbad, California, I once silently asked the question, "Why are there so many difficult people in my life?" I meditated, released the question, and began meandering through the house. My eyes scanned everything in the dining room and kitchen, but nothing spoke to me. Then in the living room my eye fell on a painting of a Greek statue, and I

was suddenly transfixed. The statue was that of a man, and across his bare chest ran several deep cracks. The cracks seemed like wounds. I *felt* the truth of it with my whole body.

In a flash I had my answer. The statue was myself! The wounds were my own! The difficult people in my life had been sent to "push my buttons," to open my emotional wounds so that I could drain the poison and heal them. Suddenly my irritation turned to gratitude as I received the gift of love and forgiveness, the realization that some of the most painful experiences in life are the greatest blessings in disguise.

What if my walk gets interrupted?

Just consider the interruption a part of your answer. If you get an emergency phone call or someone talks to you unexpectedly, pay attention. Usually it will be related to your question. Sometimes life puts interruptions in our way so we'll get the message more directly. Remember: It's all a dream. What is the distraction trying to tell you?

Can I ask more than one question at a time?

Generally it's best to ask only one. This lets you focus more clearly on your question and increases the chances of your getting a clear answer. An ideal time to ask a second question is right after the first one has been answered, when you are still in a deep meditative state. For example, after she had gotten the answer about her purpose in life, Shari might have asked, "What are some ways for me to express my love? What careers might provide ideal outlets for my love? How can I more fully express my love in my relationships? How can I live in love all the time?" Depending on how you feel, this can be done either right away or on separate Vision Walk occasions.

Is it normal to feel resistance to the Vision Walk?

Yes. In fact, a few people have told me they have enjoyed listening to my Vision Walk CD but have not done an actual walk yet. When I ask them why, some of them frankly admit that they have questions but don't want to know the answers—at least not yet.

Most people would rather be right than happy, and many people have been living a lie for so long they don't want to hear the truth. The truth can hurt, and it can also demand change. There is something in all of us that is afraid of change, even if it's for the better.

One of the scariest things ever written is the biblical statement: "You will know the truth, and the truth will make you free." People talk about freedom every day, but few are willing to admit that they are *already* free. Few are willing to take off their masks, look squarely at their lives, and admit that they have created the whole wonderful dream (or nightmare, as the case may be).

Beyond all illusions, though—including our own fear and resistance—is our ultimate fulfillment, the truth of our life, our oneness with all that is. So go ahead and ask those tough or scary questions. If you can handle the truth, the truth will make you free. . . and it will bring you more peace, love, and joy than you ever imagined.

Can I get an answer to a question I didn't ask?

Yes, this happens sometimes. When it does, it usually means that the real you has been waiting to get through to you with a message that is even more important than the question you asked. You might say the real you seizes the moment, figuring, "If I don't send the message now, he may never get it!" But in almost every case, the answer you get will also be an answer to the question you asked.

For example, one woman asked, "Shall I enroll in nursing school—yes or no?" During her first walk, she saw a hummingbird feeder. Recognizing the hummingbird as a symbol of the heart, she said to herself, "Spirit must be saying, 'Choose whatever feeds your heart.'" But she was not satisfied. The answer was not yes or no, so she asked the question again.

On her second walk, the woman saw a crucifix, which to her was a symbol of the Christ within.

Suddenly her mind put the two symbols together: "Your life is your choice. *Any* choice is the right one if it feeds your heart. Feel the Christ within, and you will make *every* choice the right one!"

Do you see how much more empowering this answer was than a simple yes or no? Your heart will never take away your power to create your own life. It will always seek to strengthen you and push you into taking more responsibility for your choices.

How can I solve problems with the Vision Walk?

Actually, there are no problems, only situations to be unraveled or left alone. All "problems" are created in the mind. Thus, it makes sense that they can be *solved* in the mind. As soon as you get out of your mind, your problems usually vanish along with your mental resistance to the situation. Here is an example:

I was "having a problem" with some friends. It was a conflict over money, and I didn't know what to do about it. So I went on a Vision Walk. I was inside a bookstore in the evening. I quieted myself and asked the question, "What is the solution to this problem?" I imagined the yellow balloon sailing off into the sky with one word written on it: "SOLUTION!" It was actually more a demand than a question, and I fully expected a solution right then and there.

After the balloon disappeared, I opened my eyes

and glided toward the bookstore entrance. In the window beside the entrance I saw a glowing, red neon sign that said, "OPEN." I thought, *Hmm, I know that has something to do with the answer, but I'm not sure what.*

I walked outside the bookstore and immediately saw an almost identical sign—"OPEN"—in the adjoining shop window. At this point, I knew that "Open" was my answer, but I didn't know how. As I continued my walk down the mall sidewalk, I passed numerous sandwich boards that had been placed in front of various shops. Each of the boards read, "OPEN." *Open . . . Open . . . Open,* I thought. Then it hit me: *Open your mind. Open your heart. Open to new possibilities. Open to your friends. Open to love. Open to life!*

By the time I got back to the bookstore a few minutes later, my problem was gone. The problem had nothing to do with my friends. It was all in my mind.

The mind has a strong tendency to create problems. It also has a strong tendency to complicate them and project them onto other people. In this way it creates even more drama and suffering, thus strengthening its false sense of identity. The ego actually *needs* problems in order to survive. Like a dog with a bone, it always has to be chewing on something. So it goes out looking for a problem, and if it can't find one it creates one. The Vision Walk is a good way of resisting this addictive temptation, getting out of your mind, and nipping problems in the bud. You may still have difficult situations to deal with after your Vision Walk, but they won't be problems unless you let your mind recreate them. And in your new frame of mind (i.e. "no-mind"), you will be able to deal with them in a much more effective way.

Will the Vision Walk work if I'm angry or upset?
Yes. In fact, doing a Vision Walk when you're in emotional turmoil is one of the best things you can do. Why? Because it forces you out of your mind and into your heart. There is no anger in your heart. There is no turmoil in your heart. Your heart is at peace all the time. Even when it is broken, deep down your heart is an endless reservoir of love and joy. You can find the real you at home there 24 hours a day. That wise, powerful no-self will give you anything you need to regain inner peace and tranquility.

What about questions that are only for personal gain?
In a way, every question you ask is for personal gain. Your deeper self is eager to give you any positive thing you could ever want. Your mind, on the other hand, will often seek things that look positive but that actually perpetuate unhappiness.

Selfish questions come from the egoic mind, which

tries to get you to believe you are separate and not enough. The ego is always trying to fill itself up with outer approval and exterior "things." The real you is not interested in things. It is not interested in whether you become rich or famous. It is only interested in your spiritual growth and the evolution of consciousness.

Sooner or later, selfish questions tend to backfire. You may become rich and famous as a result of the answers you get, but eventually you will see that riches or fame without a deep connection to life and other people is empty and unfulfilling. Even this is positive, though, because eventually your selfish questions will lead you back to the truth: We are all one—all vibrant, living cells in a massive and magnificent organism called life, and we are all held together in eternal communion by an interactive force more powerful and constant than gravity, the power of love.

How often should I do the Vision Walk?
Do it as often as you want to or need to. The main purpose of the Vision Walk is not to answer questions or solve problems; it is to get you in touch with your deeper being. Each time you do one, you will get better acquainted with the quality of your inner voice and learn a little more about how to live an authentic life.

Are any questions out of bounds?
Of course not. The universe can handle anything. It *has* no bounds; that's why it's called the universe. This is a great opportunity for *you* to practice having no boundaries. Ask anything you want. Ask the questions you think are in bounds, as well as those you think are out of bounds. Then notice the answers you get and learn for yourself what is forbidden and what is not.

How about questions motivated by anger or jealousy?
Again, ask and find out. The last thing I want to do is limit your experience or judge any question as right or wrong.

That said, my own experience is that your heart will never give you an answer that is intended to hurt anyone. Nor will it give you an answer that is intended to build your own ego. It is incapable of these things.

Your mind may *interpret* an answer in such a way that you will use it to hurt or get back at someone, but if you do this, it will come right back to you. Why? Because at the deepest level, you *are* that other person. What you see in the world is a mirror of your own inner reality.

What should I do after I get my answer?
First, realize that there are no shoulds. Anything you do or don't do is fine. But realize that your heart is talking

to you for a reason. You have opened up this channel of truth in order to improve your life, to begin drawing on the wisdom and energy of your own inner being.

Sometimes your answer will be complete in itself. Your question will have been answered or your problem solved. Something deep inside you will have changed, and there will be nothing more you need to do. At other times, your answer will ask you to make a choice or take some action. It will put your faith to the test.

If you do nothing with your answer, you will get nothing from it. If you take action, your life will begin to change. If you continue taking action, consistently following your intuition, your life will be transformed.

Taking action can be very difficult because most of our minds have created elaborate structures—complicated identities based on beliefs accumulated and practiced over many years. These beliefs are now the building blocks of who we think we are. For decades, they have kept us "safe," but they have also kept us separate, both from ourselves and others. They have determined the course of our lives, dictating what we can or cannot do.

In contrast, the answers that come to you in the Vision Walk know no structures or boundaries. Coming from the real you in the field of all possibilities, they begin to whisper (and sometimes even to shout) that you can be, do, or have almost anything you want.

Truths like this are very unsettling for the average, negatively conditioned human mind. When faced with revolutionary ideas, most minds will look for ways of ignoring or sabotaging them. Why? Because the ego is afraid of change. It wants to stay in control. It wants to keep us small and insecure. It also wants to survive. To give up resisting and controlling means death.

Be aware that your mind may not want to give up the control you have given it. The small self may fight the real you for dominion, but it is a losing battle. Deep down, there is nothing the mind wants more than to be in service to the heart. If you persevere, and especially if you honor your answers by taking action, your mind will gradually surrender its logic and knowledge—even its problems and suffering—to the peace and wisdom that abide in the deep reservoir of the real you.

Is it OK to talk about my Vision Walks?
By all means, share the wealth. But be careful whom you confide in. As your life begins to expand—as you become happier and more fulfilled, living from the inside out—you will find that some people are not overjoyed to see you changing. Even family members and close friends may have an investment in your staying the same. Don't blame them for being

normal, but don't let anyone talk you out of your inner treasure, either. If someone does, remember that it's still yours; you just need to reclaim it. Then keep your own counsel.

6

Interpreting Your Walk

U sually you will get a very clear message during your Vision Walk. You will feel the answer in your heart, and it will resonate throughout your whole body. In these cases, something inside will just say *"AHA!"* or *"YES!"* and you won't need to interpret anything; you will just *know*. At other times, the answer may require some digging. Why? Because your answers come in symbolic form, in a language your mind may not readily understand. If this happens, relax. As I said earlier, you already have the answer; you just don't know it yet.

The Vision Walk is much like a waking dream, so interpreting one is like interpreting a regular nighttime dream. Dreams often seem very confusing and complicated, but most of them are quite simple.

It's mainly a matter of figuring out the symbols.

The easiest way I know of interpreting a dream is to start with the idea that everything in it is a part of you or your life. If you dream about your brother, ask, "What part of me is my brother?" If your brother reminds you of strength and integrity, your brother in the dream represents your *own* strength and integrity. If you dream about your father or mother, those images aren't really your father or mother; they are the *energies* of your father or mother in *you*. People, paintings, birds, bugs, books, hairdryers, paperclips—literally *everything* around and inside you is a potential part of your answer. Even the things you do can be part of your answer.

Everyone who has learned to read has mental agreements about the meanings of the letters of the alphabet and their combinations into words and sentences. Likewise, your interpretation, or "reading," of a dream will depend on your understanding of these symbols and their interactions. For example, if you dream about an eagle fighting with a snake, you ask, "What does the eagle mean to me? What does the snake mean? How do I feel about their interaction?"

With the Vision Walk you do the same thing. Begin by asking yourself, "What part of me is this? What part of me is that? What does this person represent? What does that thing represent? And most important: How do I *feel* about this or that? Each person, place, or thing that catches your attention is a symbol that the real you uses to communicate something. All you have to do is figure out what it means.

Although the ultimate meaning of your dream symbols depends on you, there are some fairly universal ones that crop up all the time. For example, an automobile usually represents the physical body, a "vehicle" for the spirit. Buses often represent the emotional movement of a group of people, while a bicycle suggests a person going somewhere alone under his or her own power. Houses are where we live, so the rooms in a house often represent the various compartments or emotional "spaces" within your mind. You get the idea.

Animals can represent a wide variety of things. Each animal has its own unique message, depending on what it is doing and how you feel about it. In general, though, the animals you see in nature will represent universal archetypes. For most people the eagle represents vision and freedom. When a raven "talks" to me on a mountaintop, I know magic is afoot. When I see a hawk, I see a messenger, and usually it is a good omen. An owl, on the other hand, usually brings a warning of some kind. The hummingbird always reminds me of the heart. The rabbit represents fear, the snake transformation, the lizard the dreamer, and so on.

Go through your own animal lexicon and notice what meanings you already have stored away in your subconscious. If you want more leads about the archetypal meanings of animals, I highly recommend *Medicine Cards* by Jamie Sams and David Carson. Many of my students have found it extremely useful, both for waking and sleeping dreams.

In general, the elements of nature are quite easy to interpret. Did you notice the sky, the earth, the trees, an unusual rock, or some colorful flowers on your Vision Walk? Did they "speak" to you? What emotions did they evoke? Did you pick up a stone or a snail shell? How did you feel about them? Was there anything unusual about the weather? How did it reflect your own internal weather? Explore, continually asking yourself questions about your walk, and you will come to understand its meaning.

Practice interpreting your nighttime dreams, too. This will help a lot, because the symbols will have the same meanings for you, both in the waking and sleeping dream. One night, for example, I dreamed that I had returned from work to find a rattlesnake coiled up inside my computer printer. Having glimpsed it, I wanted only to avoid it. I started to walk away, pretending I hadn't seen it, when something prompted me to go back and look more closely.

Peering into the printer, I could clearly see the venomous reptile coiled and ready to strike. *How can I possibly get it out of there without being bitten?* I wondered. There was no immediate answer, so I just sat there eyeing the snake.

Suddenly, without warning, the snake transformed itself into a lizard. *Wow!* I thought, *That's not so threatening. Now I can probably reach in and take it out.*

Just as I reached in to grab the lizard, it changed into a crossbill, a species of finch whose beak is crossed at the end. With no prompting at all, the little bird jumped onto my wrist. As I gently lifted it out, I looked into dark, beautiful eyes as deep as the ocean and realized this bird was a gift from God.

Then I thought to myself, *I think I'll take the bird for a walk outside.* As I wandered down the street with the finch on my wrist, appreciating its beauty and fragility, it was suddenly transformed into my two-year-old boy, Travis, whom I now held lovingly in my arms.

The symbols in this dream were relatively easy to decipher. In a fairly short time, I realized that the computer represented my mind, while the printer was the part of my mind that communicates. The rattlesnake was obviously some form of mental-emotional poison that I was afraid to look at. One thing was for sure: If I didn't get it out soon, it was going to cause major problems in my communication, either with myself or others, and most likely both.

The dream told me exactly what to do: *Just pay attention and watch what happens. Watch how your own awareness transforms the emotional poisons in your mind.* As I watched, the snake became a lizard—still a cold-blooded reptile but now much smaller and no longer poisonous. To me the lizard is also the dreamer, sunning itself on warm rocks and daydreaming for hours on end. As for the crossbill, it was such a messenger of love and forgiveness that it became a living symbol of the Christ spirit itself—the gift from God that opens the doors to healing, redemption, and resurrection in all of us. Nothing, of course, could be more expressive of that resurrection and return to purity than the presence of my son, Travis, a symbol of the reunion with my own inner child.

The overall meaning of the dream? Simple: The thing you fear the most becomes the thing you love the most if you have the courage to look at it. The things that seem most poisonous in our lives—anger, hatred, guilt, regret, remorse, anxiety, and other dark shadows and limitations—can become our greatest blessings when we heal them through our loving attention and awareness.

Practice analyzing your own dreams from time to time, and you'll get better at deciphering your Vision

Walks. Books on dream interpretation can sometimes be helpful, too, but they can also mislead you. After all, it's *your* dream and they're *your* symbols. By all means, get help if you need it, but first exhaust your own inner resources. That way, you will quickly learn the infinitely creative language of the heart. You will also come to realize that beyond all the thousands of books and experts out there, you can rely on the wisdom of your own best friend and teacher—yourself!

7

Diving Deeper

Now that you have had some personal experience with the Vision Walk, you know how it works and *why* it works. You also know that the deeper purpose of the Vision Walk is to give you a taste of what it's like to be the real you.

By now you have experienced this consciousness. You know what it feels like to be in a state of quiet awareness where you have access to anything you ever wanted to know, where your problems simply vanish without effort or action, and where you feel connected to the pulse of life in a new and delightful way. You also know, if you have practiced the Vision Walk consistently, that you can extend the amount of time you spend in this state.

Maybe you have already asked yourself, "What

would my life be like if I lived in this state of consciousness all the time?" I will give you a hint. Close your eyes and picture being in love. Picture being at peace. Picture living in bliss. Picture life as an exciting adventure. Just imagine what it would be like to wake up in the morning and know there is nothing to prove, nothing to defend, no regret or anxiety, only another 24 hours full of adventures and new opportunities. Imagine what it would be like to know that you are not your body or your mind, but that you are life experiencing itself in human form.

Sound good? Well, then, why not just *be* in this state of consciousness all the time?

There are two answers to that question, and they are both very simple: habit and distraction. Most of us have spent decades developing negative beliefs *(I'm not good enough, I don't deserve, I'll never make it, I should have done this or that)* into negative thought patterns which in turn create negative patterns of emotion. These patterns have become ingrained habits. They have also taken on great momentum. Unless acted upon by an outside force, they will perpetuate themselves day after day, month after month, year after year. The real you cares nothing about these habits. It would laugh at them if it could, but most of the time our minds are making so much noise we can't even hear our still, small voice.

To make matters worse, almost everything in our

modern world conspires to pull us away from our true self and deeper into everyday drama. Television, newspapers, computers, cell phones, gossip, conflict, business meetings, harried schedules—we hardly have a moment to ourselves. But these things are all the more reason to persevere in your efforts to be the real you. Not just to cope with modern life but to rise above it.

While millions in Third World countries are besieged by disease, war, and starvation, most of the rest of us are suffering, too, though usually in less obvious ways—emotionally and spiritually. Most of us are adrift in an ocean storm, swept by the winds and tides. We feel we have little or no control over our lives. Only a small number of humans really know how to swim in the storm. These are the ones who have learned to reduce stress and flow with the currents of life. They are strong, resilient, good at "coping." Even so, they're still stuck in the storm. Only a very small percentage of those people have learned to rise above or go beyond the illusory storms of suffering altogether. We call these people masters. At first glance, we might say they have learned how to walk on water, but this is not really true. *The truth is that they have remembered they are the ocean.* Through daily discipline and practice, they have become one with the winds and tides. Now, no longer resisting the changing currents but allowing them to flow freely, they can enjoy life more than ever.

Often they can even exult in the storms!

These people are living embodiments of the true self, the real you. They are in bliss most of the time. Yet they are not special. Except for one important thing, they are just like you and me. The only real difference is their choices. More often than not, they have chosen love, peace, and joy. More often than not, they have focused on the truth. Day in and day out, they have practiced being authentic. They have awakened to their true nature. They are living embodiments of inner wisdom.

Theirs is not a superhuman feat; in fact, most of them would not call it an achievement at all. They would simply say they have let go of illusion. Masters are just people who have become fully human.

One such master is don Miguel Ruiz, author of *The Four Agreements* and *The Mastery of Love*. Yet Miguel has no interest in being seen as a master; he is interested only in awakening the master in others. And he does it with unrelenting persistence and loving ruthlessness.

One day, after I had studied with Miguel for about six years, he sat me down and said, "OK, I want you to dream. In this dream I want you to re-evaluate your relationship with me."

With Miguel seated beside me, I dutifully closed my eyes and began to "dream"—to actively meditate, visualizing and contemplating scenes from the past in order to re-evaluate the present. I went all the way back to the first time we met, to the day that magical Mexican man had greeted me at the door of his home in Santa Fe with open arms and eyes like deep, dark pools. I remembered how he'd wrapped his arms around me as though he'd known me all my life; how he'd sat me down on a couch, peered right through me, and told me bluntly, "You have too many opinions . . . and they are the wrong ones!" I remembered the many times I'd listened to Miguel teach, scribbling copious notes and hanging on his every word. I remembered our Easter gatherings and other special occasions. I remembered the restaurants, the laughter, the margaritas, the dancing. I remembered the times Miguel had publicly baited me into exposing another layer of self-importance, then ceremoniously popped my bubble in front of all my fellow apprentices. I remembered our magical trips to Teotihuacan and how he had prodded me there, too, forcing me to push beyond my self-created shackles. I even remembered how comically ruthless he was, telling me bluntly with a wry smile, "It's all your creation. Either you're happy, or you're stupid. But of course you have the right to be stupid!"

As I dreamed, Miguel put his hand on my hand, and I knew he had entered into my dream; he was right there, dreaming it all with me. As more scenes flashed before my eyes, I asked myself, *What's the common denominator here?*

Then suddenly it hit me. From the moment I had first gone to see this man, in every experience and every exchange, from start to finish, I had been doing only one thing: I had been searching for myself.

In that moment I found myself. In that moment, I realized the staggering truth: that Miguel and I were one. Not theoretically, not partly, not almost—no, literally and completely. Just beneath the thin façade of minds, bodies, and personal histories, we were *literally* one and the same. After all my searching and struggling, I had found myself at last, in the crystal-clear mirror of my own beloved teacher.

Tears of quiet joy began streaming down my cheeks. As I opened my eyes and looked into Miguel's eyes, he squeezed my hand and said softly but intently, "Yes, it's true: You are me. I am you. . . . And there is more!"

It was so like Miguel not to tempt my self-importance or to let me rest on my laurels for even a second. It took me a long time to realize the "more," but in the end it wasn't anything I hadn't known before. Once you realize it for yourself, it's the most obvious thing in the world: At the deepest level, we are not only each other, we are *everything*.

Of course, realizing the truth and living it

consistently are two different things. In spite of many marvelous glimpses of the truth—even after spending weeks so deeply immersed in it that I hardly knew or cared where "Brandt" had gone and couldn't feel regret or anxiety if I tried—I have fallen prey to illusion and had to pick myself up again. So goes the dance between the drop and the ocean. The fact remains, though, we all have the seeds of truth inside us. Any one of us can become a master. More to the point, we already are. Most of us are masters of drama and suffering, masters of doubt and fear, masters of whatever we have practiced all our lives. We can become *awakened* masters—masters of a new way of perceiving and living—anytime we choose.

How? First by letting go of the idea that such mastery is unattainable. Second, by wanting it more than anything. And third and most important, by practicing—that is, acting as if we already had it (which, of course, we do!)

Wherever you may be on your path, and whatever your life's dream may be, there are things you can do to deepen your sense of mastery and awaken the truth that is already in you. Here are 10 simple suggestions. I offer them not as a system or program, but only as tools that have been helpful on my own path.

1. **Develop a daily spiritual practice.** This might

include meditation, prayer, a candlelight ritual, a few moments of devotion at your altar—almost anything to affirm the truth of who you are. In this practice, make it a point to turn off your mind. I like to start the day with a walk or a swim followed by an hour of yoga and meditation. Some of my students say affirmations. Others focus on prayer. Some spend only a few minutes, others up to two hours. The time isn't as important as the regularity and sincerity with which you do it—especially when you don't feel like it.

2. **Take relaxation breaks throughout the day.** Take a walk in nature. Breathe in the fresh air. Feel the love and life in each breath. As you breathe, express your gratitude for being alive. Marvel at the miracle of life— the trees, the birds and butterflies, your fellow humans, even the bustling traffic. Make sure each break leaves you feeling peaceful and refreshed.

3. **Be here now.** This moment is the only one you have, the only one that's real. Past and future are only figments of the imagination. Be here now. Focus completely on what you're doing in this moment, not on what happened in the past or what might happen in the future. Avoid worry and regret and other emotions that pull you away from the Now. Yes, you have to plan for the future, but plan right now—without worrying.

Ideally, plan knowing and feeling with every fiber of your being that it's already done.

In trying times, do your best to stay grounded. Instead of running away from emotional discomfort, be present with it. If you feel angry or upset, notice the feeling but don't make it into a story. Really *feel* the feeling and watch what happens. Instead of judging, blaming, or projecting negative emotions, ask yourself, "Who's talking?" Is it the deeper self or the programmed robot? When you realize it's the program, suddenly you're seeing through the eyes of the master again. You are the silent watcher, fully present in the moment. As the watcher, you can make a conscious choice, and that choice will always be love.

4. **Work with a spiritual mentor.** This can be anyone you admire and respect, from an ancient master to a living spiritual teacher. Though it will probably speed your progress, it isn't necessary to study directly with this master; the important thing is to use him or her as a mirror to reflect the master within *you*. Place your mentor's photograph on your altar. Listen carefully to his or her words. Read books, listen to tapes, and attend workshops. Absorb and emulate your mentor's spirit. Nourish yourself daily with the truths this master has to share. In time you will discover that you embody those same truths. Why? Because, like the flames of a

brightly burning fire, a good mentor is someone who warms your soul and awakens the light of truth that is already in you.

5. **Let go of judgments.** Have you ever noticed how your judgments bring you down and separate you from other people? Letting go of judgments is one of the most freeing things you can do. First become aware of your judgments. Start by making a list of all the judgments you have about family members, friends, lovers, institutions, groups of people, and yourself. Continue by noting all the judgments you make during a single day. (During my apprenticeship with Miguel, he had me speak every judgment into a pocket tape recorder, and it seemed like that was all I did for several days.) Keep this up for at least a month. Just the act of paying attention begins to break the habit. Over time, your judgments will become less severe and less frequent. You will also become a much more peaceful and loving human being.

6. **Forgive yourself and others.** Most of us shrink away from the idea of forgiveness because there doesn't seem to be any justice in it. Why should we forgive someone who did us wrong? The answer is that it doesn't make any difference whether a person deserves to be forgiven or not. We forgive because we don't want to

carry that old poison around anymore. We forgive not for the other, but for ourselves. Forgiveness is an act of self-love.

Take inventory of all the people and situations you need to forgive. (Hint: look at the list you made for the previous exercise.) Write them all down on paper. If you don't know what needs to be forgiven, ask what people and situations are draining your energy. Again, be sure to include yourself. Next, devise a ritual that will clean all this negative energy out of your body.

Rituals bypass the mind, going straight to the heart and the hidden pockets of poison in the body. Some people imagine they are talking with the person in question. Others write letters of forgiveness and burn them. Still others set photos or symbols adrift on a river or lake or get their whole bodies involved by doing ritual dances of forgiveness. As with the Vision Walk, follow your heart. You never know what it will come up with. Not knowing why at first, one woman I know took a walk in the woods and wound up giving her grievances to a tree. Another stripped off her clothing, slathered herself in raspberries, then took a shower and dressed all in white. Consult your own intuition. Whatever has power for *you* is what you should do. If you do it sincerely, you're sure to feel like a great weight has been lifted from you. (For more on forgiveness, see the section on "The Breath of

Forgiveness" in Chapter 8, The Toltec Path.

7. **Practice unconditional gratitude.** Most of us find it easy to give thanks for the "good" things in life—families, friends, and good fortune—but few of us find it easy to give thanks for the so-called "bad" things. The kind of gratitude I'm talking about here is unconditional. That's right, I'm suggesting that you give thanks for *everything*. This kind of gratitude teaches you how to live constantly appreciating life as it is, not as you want it to be. There is no way you can suffer when you're saying yes to life. Gratitude also bypasses the need for forgiveness. If you go straight into gratitude after someone does you wrong, there is nothing to forgive. The mastery of gratitude is the ultimate expression of personal freedom because it honors all that you are and all that happens to you while respecting the freedom of others to make their own choices.

8. **Surrender to the real you.** Surrender is not losing; it is winning. Surrender is not giving up; it is giving over. Give over your burdens, give over your ego, give over your grievances, give over the baggage of the past. Surrender is handing over to the real you all that is not you.

Ever hefted a full, 39-gallon plastic garbage bag?

Imagine what it would be like carrying that around all day. Yet that's what most of us are doing—carrying huge black bags of mental and emotional garbage. It's exhausting. Yet not only do we carry it, we don't want to give it up. About the only time we put it down is to open the bag and share the stinky stuff with our friends. ("Hey, you won't believe what John did to me yesterday! . . . Did you hear about what my ex-wife said? . . . Look what else I've got in my bag. . . . What have you got in yours?")

We complain endlessly, telling our victim stories, then ask our friends to share theirs. Through gossip, our burdens get even heavier. But give up the weight of all this juicy stuff? No way! The heavier the baggage, the more invested we seem to get. It's almost as if the things we're carrying have become what we think we are. But if we have the courage to surrender—to drop that baggage like a hot coal and never look back— there's a new world waiting for us. A much lighter world, a much brighter and happier world.

You can surrender in your morning prayers, in a traffic jam, or in an argument with an enemy. You can surrender at an altar, a steering wheel, a tree, or a telephone pole. At any moment, you can give up your need to be right, your need to protect and defend, your need to be recognized as important or powerful or loving or good (or bad, for that matter).

In any moment, you can turn over your ego's needs and rest in peace and humility. In that moment, your whole world changes. You lose what never had value in the first place and gain what has everlasting value. You give up being a servant of suffering and become a servant of love.

9. **Love unconditionally.** There is nothing as powerful as love. Love is the primordial impulse that created the universe and the glue that holds it together. Love is the bedrock of your being. If you invoke the spirit of love and allow it to take over your life, it will speed you toward freedom faster than any technique or tool you could possibly devise. When I say, "Love unconditionally," what I mean is just that: Love without conditions of any kind. Start by loving yourself, just the way you are—no judgments or expectations and no strings attached. Continue by loving your family and friends, just the way they are. Then extend your love to your neighbors, co-workers, community— then strangers and even your adversaries or enemies. Imagine the last thing you would want to do is try to change anybody. Pretend they are all God in disguise, playing just the role intended for them to play. Why? Because at the core of your being, love is what you are. It's what everyone else is, too. Regardless of how much that love may be twisted or distorted, that's the stuff

we're all made of. Each time you share your love, it grows stronger. Each time you give it away, it comes back. Each time it comes back, it grows bigger. As it grows bigger, it liberates you to live more from the truth. (For more specifics on loving unconditionally, see "The Self-Love Mirror Exercise" in Chapter 8, The Toltec Path.)

10. **"Just be oh-so-happy."** First let me explain where this one comes from: More than a decade ago, I was getting ready to go to Teotihuacan, Mexico, the birthplace of the Toltec tradition, with don Miguel for the first time. Two months before the journey, I asked him enthusiastically, "Miguel, what can I do to prepare for Teo? I'll do anything you say. Should I learn Spanish? Read up on the ruins? Learn about the old masters?" Miguel just chuckled and said, "No, no—none of those things. Just be oh-so-happy!"

You wouldn't think that such a simple suggestion could have much effect, much less transform your life. Think again. When you're happy, you're positive, outgoing, and open to the best that life has to offer, whether you're at home or in Teotihuacan or Timbuktu. Most people are looking for reasons to justify their *un*happiness, and they find them. You can reverse that expectation and get the same results. Imagine what your life would be like if "Thou shalt be happy" were a commandment from God and you wanted to do everything in your power to follow it. You would be looking everywhere for excuses to be happy, and you would find them. You would find happiness where others found sadness, blessings where others found curses.

When you're really awake, happiness is a choice. So go ahead and try it. What have you got to lose? Decide to be a happy, positive, fun-loving person. Act as if it were true, and notice what happens. A good way to start is by cultivating your sense of humor. Start by letting go of all those cares and worries. Relax, loosen up, laugh loudly and often. Laughter is such powerful medicine that, in addition to Miguel's book, *The Four Agreements* (one of which is *Don't take anything personally*), I recommend a "Fifth Agreement": *Don't take anything seriously.*

So there you have 10 simple tools that can help you on your spiritual path. Finally, I would like to offer a few suggestions to go with the tools.

One is to beware of spiritual addiction. I say this because many amazing, magical things can and do happen on the spiritual path, and it's easy to get attached to them. Once you've taken a spirit journey to the stars or met a master in your dreams, it's tempting to feel special, somehow more spiritually adept, and want to blab it all over creation. Once you've talked with a tree or flown to the sun or merged with a manatee, it's tempting to want more—even to think that when you're feeling merged and high all the time you will have arrived. Nothing could be further from the truth. That just perpetuates never getting there. That just makes you a spiritual experience junkie. It's a big distraction. The real value in any path is not in mystical experiences or spiritual escapism but being able to bring your newfound wisdom down to earth and live it every day.

Not that these experiences aren't wonderful and don't have value; they certainly do. But daily life is where the rubber meets the road. The truth is, you have already arrived; you may just not know it yet. There is nowhere to go, nothing to do. No different state or place or time than the one you're in right now will take you any closer to heaven than you already are. You can merge and take ecstatic flights until you're green in the face, and you won't be any more free than you are right now. Liberation isn't in spiritual experiences; it's in detaching from the incessant chatter of the mind.

Which reminds me: The chatter of the mind is very good at creating emotional pain and suffering. In fact, that's what it does best. Most of us want—or at least *say* we want—to avoid suffering, but seldom do we look at the motivational value it has. For many people, suffering is the thing that pushed them onto the spiritual path in the first place. For others, it's the main motivation for continuing. When you're in pain, you want to get out of it. When you're suffering—that is, resisting what is—you have an even bigger reason to be free. When the suffering gets unbearable, you may suddenly drop it because it's too heavy to carry anymore.

If you're not so invested in resistance, you may not need to suffer much. If you're half awake already, it may be much easier to be present with your pain and work through it rather than running away from it. Being present with your pain is usually a gentler way of finding freedom, but it isn't the only way. There isn't any right or wrong way. The right way is *your* way. So do it your way. Don't judge how it *"should"* be done. It makes little difference whether you work to dissolve your suffering by being present and aware, or whether you drop it because you can't carry it anymore. Either way, you use life's pains and problems as stepping stones. Either way, you come to the truth by way of your illusions. Either way you're free of suffering in the end . . . just as long as you don't pick it up again. The following chapter has much more to say about all this.

8

The Toltec Path

As I mentioned earlier, when I first met don Miguel Ruiz in the spring of 1994, he sat me down on a couch, scrutinized me silently for about 15 seconds, and announced flatly, "You have too many opinions. . . And they are the wrong ones!"

I was surprised and confused. Up until that moment, I had thought that my opinions and beliefs were sacred, the very foundation of my integrity and my life as a unique human being.

Miguel seemed to be reading my mind. "Opinions are not right or wrong or good or bad," he said, "but you need to look at them and find out which ones work for you and which ones do not work. Your beliefs can make you happy, or they can make you miserable. They can create the most beautiful relationships, or they can destroy your connection to the ones you love the most. They can bring you lots of money and success, or they can sabotage everything you do. What you need to do is look at your beliefs. When you find the ones that work, keep them. When you find ones that don't work, throw them in the trash!"

I had never heard of anything so radical. I was dumbfounded at the simplicity of it. I argued that it couldn't be that simple, but Miguel would hear nothing of it. He insisted that if I wanted to be free from suffering, this is what I needed to do.

At the end of our interview, Miguel ushered me to the door saying, "There is no need to complicate it. Your job is to take the power out of the opinions. That is enough for now. We will start with that. When you are done, we will go on to something else."

I suspect Miguel was chuckling when I left, because we never got to the next thing. After more than six years on the Toltec path, I realized that *was* the Toltec path. Everything we did was about "taking the power out of the opinions"—paying attention to thoughts and emotions, challenging old beliefs, dismantling personal and social conditioning, demolishing my very concept of who I was. As time went by, I began to realize that the "I" I thought I was, was nothing more than a bundle of socially conditioned thoughts, ideas, opinions, and beliefs that were creating automatic emotional reactions. I was little more than a computer-programmed robot. The Toltec path was a deconstruction project!

I spent hours, days, weeks, and months examining my opinions and beliefs and asking which were true and which were false. I noticed which ones made me happy and which ones made me miserable. As I became more aware of the limiting beliefs that ran my life, they began to soften and fall away. As they did, I began to feel freer, happier. I even began to go through periods when I didn't believe anything. Those periods became increasingly frequent, and they brought me deep peace and joy. They still do.

What is true doesn't have to be believed. Anyone who frees himself from the prison of the mind—even for a few moments—knows from experience what lies beyond the confines of belief. There you will find passion and creativity. There you will find wildness and wisdom. There you will find a deep reservoir of love, peace, and joy—your true nature, the real you.

Of course, the Toltec path is not *the* path; it is only one among many that lead to the top of the same mountain. No matter what our religion or spiritual tradition, we are all seeking the truth. We are all seeking love, peace, joy, and freedom from suffering. Yet so many of us spend decades seeking and never finding. *The aim of the Toltec path is to become a finder.* Then, when you have reached the top of the mountain, there is no more path.

The Toltec path uses a wide variety of tools to help seekers become finders. Among them are some rich and powerful mythologies. The most common is the mythology of the parasite, a mean, nasty beast that sucks your energy by manipulating your thoughts and emotions. Another is that of the black magician, the inner saboteur who is always casting dark spells and destroying your own and others' most cherished dreams. A third is the idea of being trapped in a prison of social conditioning where the bricks of the prison walls are your limiting beliefs, held together by the mortar of faith. As you examine the bricks, you shine the light of your consciousness on them, melting the mortar and pushing the bricks out one by one until the prison walls collapse.

These are all wonderful mythologies. However, it is important to understand that they are not the truth; they are only signs pointing to the truth. It is important not to become a worshipper of signposts.

With this proviso, I would like to add another mythology that came in a dream years ago to a fellow apprentice named Gayle Dawn Price. Gayle Dawn dreamed that all of us were being held captive in a concrete dungeon. Though it was modern, the dungeon was dark and dank, not unlike the castle dungeons of old, with creepy corridors reaching in many directions and ghastly dangers lurking everywhere. Fires or floods could erupt at any time. Worst of all, the entire dungeon was under surveillance by armed guards with bows and arrows, and they were constantly trying to shoot us with steel-tipped poison arrows.

"The rules were very strict," Gayle Dawn explained. "If a guard managed to shoot you and the arrow struck, you would immediately be yanked up to the ceiling by ropes around both ankles and left hanging there upside-down until the guards decided you had suffered enough to let you down."

I had no trouble imagining the agony of hanging for hours by my ankles with an arrow stuck in my belly or back.

"On the other hand," Gayle Dawn went on, "if a guard shot at you and you were fast enough to snatch the arrow out of midair before it stuck, you could take the arrow to the guardhouse and buy your freedom."

There you have it—the entire Toltec path in a neat little nutshell. It's all about buying your freedom. Permanent freedom. Not freedom from corruption or crime or an oppressive government. Not freedom from life's challenges or difficult people or anything outside yourself. No. What I'm talking about is *freedom from the tyranny of your own mind.*

Let's take a closer look at the dream symbols. The

dungeon is what the Toltecs often call the "dream of the planet," the pits, a place very much like hell where most of us spend our days just getting by, or worse. Most of the time we don't even know we're in hell because it's so normal. The guards are our mental programs, our "parasites," the ones who both generate and feed on emotional poison in order to maintain themselves and the oppressive environment. These guards are both inside us and outside. Just like the mechanized agents in the movie, *The Matrix,* they patrol our mental-emotional reality, milking their human hosts for energy and staying constantly on the lookout for inmates who are trying to escape.

The arrows are the poisonous thoughts that come either from ourselves or others. Their effect is devastating, creating anger, frustration, fear, guilt, regret, remorse, anxiety, depression, and a host of other symptoms that all add up to a living hell. We all know what it feels like to be in our own personal hell. And every day we hear about the collective effect of all this insanity on the six o'clock news.

It's true, most of us *are* stuck in a concrete dungeon. Everywhere we turn, it seems, people and life situations are shooting poison arrows at us. Even more commonly, we're shooting at ourselves. The arrows are flying everywhere. As soon as an arrow finds its mark, our lives are turned upside-down. One moment we're peaceful and calm, the next we're dangling from the rafters, feeling the poison spreading through our entire bodies. Sometimes a single, well-aimed shot—even from a loved one—can keep us hung up for days.

Once we're strung up, the only way down is to pull out the arrow and let the poison wear off. But instead, we often nurse the poison and spread it to others by shooting more arrows—arrows of anger, gossip, retribution, self-blame, guilt, revenge, and umpteen other forms of fear and loathing. Then the situation gets worse. Whole communities can get hung up, even whole nations.

As Gayle Dawn pointed out, though, the good news is that we can buy our freedom. If we're aware enough and quick enough, we can dodge the arrows. If we're *really* quick, we can deflect or catch them before they even reach us. Even if we're not fast enough, we can still pull out the arrow, drop it, and let the poison wear off. The Toltec path is about becoming so aware that your rejection of emotional poison—either your own or someone else's—is automatic. Awareness buys you immunity from suffering. If it's strong enough, it frees you from the dungeon forever. Then you can go back and free others.

How do you get out of the dungeon? As anyone knows who has escaped from a prison of any kind, first you have to want it. You've got to have the desire. The desire usually comes through some form of suffering. You get to a point where you're fed up with it. Then you start planning. You learn everything you can about the guards and what makes them tick. You watch their every move. You notice when they shoot at you and why you're vulnerable to their attack. *You become a master of awareness.*

That is to say, you start planning your escape by becoming aware of what's going on inside you. You pay attention. You notice what you feel. You notice what you think. You notice how certain thoughts create certain emotions. You notice your habit patterns, addictions, desires, and revulsions. You notice the voice of the judge and the victim and the beliefs that fuel their voices. You also begin to notice that whatever you believe comes true, and that what you believe is creating your entire life's dream. You discover that, as Deepak Chopra puts it, "We think things are just happening to us, but at a very primordial level we are *making* them happen."

The most important thing you notice is that you are the one who is doing it. You clearly see that your beliefs are creating the whole dream. You don't like what you see, but you know you're creating it. At this point, you begin to take responsibility for your life. At this point, the gates to the prison start to open.

As you become a master of awareness, you also

begin to notice something about the poison arrows: The ones that hurt the most are the ones that reopen old wounds—usually wounds you'd forgotten you had. Wounds you'd swept under the rug. Wounds that are festering with beliefs about the way life should be (but isn't).

If you're a true master of awareness, you can even be grateful when you get shot. After all, how are you going to know what wounds you have unless they're activated? After you're shot, you can pull out the arrow, heal the wound, and wash the old belief down the drain. Once you've dissolved the energy that maintained the wound, that arrow can't touch you again. Or next time it will go right through you. After you've done this enough times, or gotten good enough to catch an arrow in midair (remember in *The Matrix* when Neo finally manages to stop a hail of bullets with his bare hands?) you can go to the guardhouse and buy your freedom.

There are many tools for healing wounds and throwing old beliefs in the trash. Like Miguel, however, I want to keep it very simple. So I am going to pass on two of the most powerful Toltec tools I know and suggest that you practice them and see how they work for you. (Then maybe we'll go on to something else.)

The Breath of Forgiveness

Traditional Toltecs call this the *recapitulation breath.* Whatever you call it, it's astonishingly effective for releasing old wounds, detaching from old programs, and banishing negative beliefs. I have simplified it somewhat, but these are the basics:

Begin by sitting in a comfortable position, either in a chair or on the floor, and closing your eyes. Identify a person or event that is causing you suffering—someone or something to which you have given your energy or power and which has left you feeling some form of negativity or discomfort. Imagine this person or event, and set your intent to clear the energy surrounding it. You might begin by calling on your higher self, asking your guides for help, or saying a quiet prayer. Prayer is always a powerful activity. It immediately humbles you, quiets the mind, and opens the door to the real you, the source of all healing.

When you are ready, take a deep breath in through your nose as you turn your head all the way to the left. As you breathe in to the left, imagine yourself drawing back all the power and energy you gave to this person or event. Then, breathing out through your mouth, turn your head all the way to the right, releasing any darkness or negativity you have taken on from the person or event. As you breathe out, bless the person or event, releasing everything you have been holding onto in the spirit of forgiveness. Imagine the darkness dissipating like a smoke or a storm cloud in the wind, or seeping into the earth or the sun to be recycled into the pure light of truth. Then bring your head back to the center and notice how you feel.

Repeat this breath as many times as it takes to clear the image or feeling of stuckness. Then go on to the next image or feeling. Like most things, this exercise will gain power and effectiveness with practice. After a while, you will instinctively know what to work on, and your body will tell you what to do next.

Start with 15 minutes a day. When you see how effective it is, you may want to become more systematic about it, increasing the time to 30 minutes a day. You may even want to make a list of all the people and events in your life and embark on a long-term program of "erasing personal history." When you're no longer attached to your life story with all its traumas and dramas and judgments and complaints, you no longer see yourself as a separate human being with the need to protect and defend and be right all the time. Your mind begins to soften and let down its guard. Before you know it, you discover you're no longer attached to being you, and there *are* no more guards. You are free from the dungeon, free from the prison of social conditioning. You have "taken the power out of the opinions."

The Breath of Forgiveness doesn't have to be done just with people or events; it can also be done with concepts, beliefs, and ideas that are keeping you stuck. Just feel the effect of the negative belief that has sapped your energy, take back your power as you breathe in to the left, and release the belief's hold on you as you breathe out to the right. Do this for 15 to 30 minutes a day on a regular basis, and you will be amazed at how fast you can clear old patterns and heal old wounds.

The Power of Self-Love

There are three steps to healing a festering wound: open it up, clean out the poison, then dress it and take care of it. In the Toltec tradition, you open the wound with the truth, you clean it out with forgiveness, and you heal it up with self-love. We have already talked about the first two steps. Now I want to talk about the third.

One of the things I routinely do in my Toltec apprenticeship program is to help people identify their core beliefs—the one root conviction on which their identity hinges and that most profoundly affects every area of their lives. Surprisingly, about 95 percent of the time, that core belief is *I'm not good enough.* That's right—about 19 out of 20 people believe they're unworthy and unlovable. Even when they are outwardly very successful, most people have a weak or damaged sense of self-esteem. There are many powerful tools for attaining personal freedom, but none of them will work as long as there is a festering wound of unworthiness. I know of no antidote more powerful for healing this wound than self-love.

Someone might argue that self-love is narcissistic, but that is not the kind of love I'm talking about. What I'm talking about is just the opposite—the kind of love that leads not only to self-acceptance but to love and respect for everyone else, to embracing life and taking a healthy place in the human community. Just look at a few of the benefits of this kind of love:

If you truly love yourself unconditionally, you will automatically be impeccable with your word. You will be unable to criticize or abuse yourself, and you will not tolerate abuse from anyone else. When you truly love yourself, you will be immune to the dream of the planet and all its drama and pain. You will be immune to gossip and anger and poison of all kinds. Things people say about you will not bother you. You will be able to really listen and learn from others, but there will be nothing in you that will accept their poison. You will no longer shoot arrows at yourself, and the arrows others shoot at you will turn into flowers before they can even touch you.

Your world and everyone in it is a mirror for how you feel about yourself. When you have unloving thoughts or feelings about yourself, you automatically project them onto others. When you truly love yourself, you project unconditional love onto others. The love you send out will come back to you many times over.

When you truly love yourself, you will have more compassion for others. You will see not only how everyone else is a mirror for you, but how everyone else is a part of you. Eventually, you will look into other people's eyes and see the same love you are sending them coming back to you.

When you love yourself, you will no longer need to defend, protect, or justify yourself in any way. You will easily forgive yourself your mistakes and transgressions as learning experiences, and you will more easily forgive others their transgressions against you. You will not feel self-important or separate or less than anyone else, because you will not need to create false impressions in order to be loved by others. It will not matter whether you are loved by others, because the love coming from you will be all that you need. The constant expression of your own love will both heal and sustain you every day of your life.

When you truly love yourself, you will have very little other work to do on any path. Everything else will come easily. You will feel your eternal connection with the Creator, you will know that you deserve fulfillment and abundance without struggle, and you will do those things that create only the highest good for yourself and others.

There are many more reasons for loving yourself, yet so few people have mastered it. How do you do it? Is there a miracle pill? Is there a shortcut? Is it really possible to reach such a state of love for yourself that childhood wounds and social conditioning magically disappear?

Usually it takes some work, but it actually *is* a little like magic. You have probably had a taste of it already. Paying attention to your judgments and emotions is a very powerful act of self-love. As you begin to shine the light of truth on your conditioned beliefs—as you begin to see the self-created prison of your own thoughts and emotions—your old wounds begin to surface. It happens automatically. It is like pouring clean, clear water into a glass of muddy water. Gradually the muddy water is replaced by the clear water. This process is not painless; it hurts to expose old wounds. But you can forgive painful events and heal old wounds much more quickly with love. And it is much easier if you relax and surrender to the process. Just remember, truth exposes the wound, forgiveness cleans it out, and love heals it up. The more love you have for yourself, the more easily and quickly you will heal your past.

So how do you love yourself unconditionally,

especially when you may have spent decades thinking you're not good enough, not perfect enough, unworthy of fulfillment, dependent on the opinions of others, or any number of other limiting thoughts? The same way you learned *not* to love yourself: through repetition, through daily practice. By doing it. You learn to love yourself by *acting* as though you loved yourself, even when you don't believe it. Even though you may believe you are unworthy or unlovable, when you act as though you were lovable, you begin to *feel* more lovable. Through repeated thought and action, you trick your mind into believing something different. Before long, the new belief is stronger than the old one, and you have created a new habit.

You can do this with any belief, but there is no more worthwhile belief to internalize than unconditional love for yourself. The unfortunate fact is that most of us go through rituals of self-deprecation every day, from the moment we wake up until the moment we go to sleep—and even in our dreams the litany continues: Not good enough, pretty enough, smart enough. Made a mistake, should have said this, should have done that. The internal dialogue is an automatic replay of all the things we have come to practice and believe about ourselves for sometimes half a lifetime. As an Eastern mystic put it, "The human mind is a most amazing thing. Every day it thinks 60,000 thoughts. And an even more amazing thing is that the very next day it thinks exactly the *same* 60,000 thoughts!"

Realizing these entrenched thought patterns, here are some things you can do every day to dilute the self-loathing and strengthen the self-love:

1. **The Self-Love Mirror Exercise.** Each morning or evening (preferably both), spend at least 10 minutes in front of a mirror—full length and in the nude, if possible—looking at your own reflection. Notice what you like and don't like about yourself. Notice the judgments that come up, even when you judge yourself for judging. Then radiate love toward your reflection. Smile at yourself and say, "I love you, _____" (and add your name), even if you don't believe it. In fact *especially* if you don't believe it. Repeat out loud all the loving, supportive thoughts you can think of. This may feel awkward, narcissistic, or silly at first. If you hear a voice of protest, simply smile and say, "I love you" again . . . and again . . . and again, until you see a glint of truth in your eyes and you know you have actually begun to believe it. Remember, we're pushing the envelope here, stepping out of the comfort zone. If you stick with this and do it often enough, it will become a habit,

and eventually you will feel your own love being reflected back to you. You will begin to laugh and lighten up. Before long, you will begin to see through the social masks, hear the love in the words you are speaking, and unconditionally welcome your new reflection. Remember, this is not narcissism or selfishness. This is one of the most selfless things you do. True selfishness is *not* loving yourself. If you practice, it can transform all your relationships and ultimately your entire world.

2. **Odd-Moment Affection.** During the day at odd moments, think of how much you love yourself and smile. Imagine wrapping your arms around yourself as though you were the most precious person in the world. Imagine loving everyone else in the same way, and begin projecting that love to those around you. Project it all the time—at home, while you're driving, while you're at work, standing in the checkout line. Imagine having the belief, "I love everyone all the time." Repeat it like a mantra. Repeat it with feeling and notice what a difference it makes, how it grows on you—how true it really is! Imagine looking at the people around you and thinking what wonderful expressions of

life they all are. Imagine loving your enemies in the same way you love yourself and notice how you feel. Project and look for the reflection of love as you go through your day, and notice what happens.

3. **Congratulate and Appreciate.** Take time to congratulate yourself on a job well done. Take time to appreciate all that you do for others—your mate, your children, your community, yourself. Be grateful for your body, your mind, your emotions and senses—this amazing vehicle through which you can experience the splendor and magic of life on Planet Earth.

4. **Take Positive, Loving Action.** Do thoughtful, loving things for yourself each day. Buy yourself flowers, light a candle, enjoy a long bath, get a massage, treat yourself to a delightful dinner, take time to relax and meditate. Enjoy everything you do, and make everything you do a ritual of love.

5. **Read Inspiring Books.** Read books and listen to tapes and CDs that will enhance the vibration of love that is your natural state. Expose yourself to expressions that will strengthen

your self-love and the truth of who you are. Some of my favorites are *The Four Agreements* and *The Mastery of Love*, by Miguel Ruiz; *Loving What Is*, by Byron Katie; *The Power of Now*, by Eckhart Tolle; and *Excuse Me, Your Life is Waiting*, by Lynn Grabhorn. To these I would add the books and recordings of Adyashanti and Francis Lucille, two eloquent expressions of the spirit of oneness.

There are many other things you can do to cultivate self-love. Just remember that your relationship with yourself is no different from your relationship with your partner, children, friends, and others—even nature and the earth. In fact, it is usually a mirror image of those other relationships. If you ever wonder what's wrong with your relationship with you, just take a look at your relationships with the others in your life, and vice versa.

As you love yourself more and more, you will find that your other relationships begin to change. You will no longer be bothered by the critical thoughts, words, or deeds of others. You will no longer be plagued by guilt, regret, or fear of failure. You will be more creative and playful. Your inner child (and your outer children) will feel happier and more secure. You will enjoy your life more in the moment because you are always with the one you love.

Love heals all wounds. It's the most powerful force on the planet, and it's right inside you. Your own love can open doors to a joy and peace you may never have imagined possible.

Not of This World

You may have gathered from the mythologies mentioned that the Toltec solution to world peace is not to change the world, only to change yourself. Each person who frees himself from suffering becomes a clear expression of love and peace, a lit candle that can light other candles. You can help to dispel the darkness in others just by being the real you. And that flame can spread all around the world.

The truth of who you are is beyond any belief, any story, any mythology. It is also beyond any concept of self. Even self-love is like a set of training wheels to keep you upright on your bike until you ride *beyond* self-love into the universal love that you are. In that place there *is* no more "you," just pure awareness watching and enjoying the show.

Recently, one of my students expressed the feeling that he was going nowhere fast. "Congratulations," I said. "That's what the Toltec path is all about."

All spiritual paths are going nowhere, some faster than others. When all our stories fall away, there is no more path. In a way, "the spiritual path" is just a big game to give the mind something to chew on. Ironically, when the mind gets out of the way, suddenly you're home. The four-lane highway dead-ends in the middle of your own living room, just where you've always been.

This is why the Toltec path emphasizes "crushing self-importance" and "erasing personal history." Once your story is gone, so is the person you thought you were. And in the place of that imposter, the simple truth is staring you in the face. You are free. You are happy. You love everyone just as they are. You love life just as it is, just as it presents itself day by day, hour by hour, minute by minute. When you detach from your concept of who you are supposed to be, you become passionately attached to the present moment. And that moment is shifting all the time. You don't need to hold on anymore.

In this state of no-mind, you don't want to change anyone or anything. You love everyone just as they are. You love even those who misunderstand you and persecute you and call you their enemy. The real you has no enemies. You can't help loving them—not because you are special or some kind of saint, but because you are so simple and ordinary. Because you know there isn't any us and them and never was. *Because you know they are you.*

In this state of no-mind, everything around you gives you pleasure. Just to be alive gives you pleasure. Just to contemplate the wonder of another day on Planet Earth gives you pleasure. Just to open your eyes in the morning and see the sunlight streaming through the window. Just to smell a flower or see a smile. To watch a bird taking a bath. Even to stroll across a parking lot. When you have finally gotten nowhere, everything is a wonder to behold. Everything is just life experiencing itself. And the one who is looking through your eyes is no longer the "you" you thought you were. *It's you as life, you as pure awareness.*

This doesn't mean you don't have preferences. This doesn't mean you don't have goals and dreams or don't care about anything; quite the contrary. The no-thing expresses itself uniquely through each form—every flower, every bird, every fish, every human—so there are always going to be preferences and differences and wondrously varied expressions. It's just that you're no longer *attached* to those preferences. You don't have to have it your way anymore. You don't have to be right anymore. You don't have to be admired or respected or loved or hated anymore in order to be you. You don't have to create a drama in order to feel alive. In this state, there is no more you to have it your way. There *is* no more you to be right anymore. You no longer identify with your identity.

When you no longer identify with your identity, all your attachments fall away. All your concepts fall away. Even all your beliefs fall away. In a way, you don't even have preferences anymore. Instead of preferring this over that, or that over this, paradoxically you prefer everything. You don't hate yourself anymore, and you don't love yourself anymore. There is no more self to love or hate. You have left the dream of the planet behind. You are not of this world.

"But what about real life?" you may ask. "In such a state of no-self, isn't it impossible to function in the real world?" Not at all. Paradoxically (and this is a real kicker), it gets even better. Far from being an airy-fairy personage completely divorced from the "real" world, your becoming "not of this world" propels you even *more* into the world. When you become more detached from your little self, you become even more effective, more passionate, more compassionate, more loving, more committed, more down to earth than ever before. When that poor little suffering self disappears, you can take even bigger risks, live even more fully and completely. Why? Because you're no longer afraid. Not afraid of criticism, not afraid of not being loved, not afraid of being hated, not afraid of making a mistake or being wrong, not afraid of death, not even afraid of life. You're just not afraid. You're free. Free to love, free to live, free to lap up every moment like a loyal dog, knowing each moment is a gift, knowing that moment is all you have, and trusting that that moment is all you need. And like a dog that's had its paws on the steering wheel far too long, you're perfectly content just to curl up in the back seat, sniff the air, watch the passing scenery, and leave the driving to life.

It doesn't matter if you're a parent with a hundred responsibilities or a student holding down two jobs, or a corporate CEO—and especially if you're a person other people look to to solve their problems—there comes a time when a shift in consciousness is the path your heart must take. Not long ago a friend of mine came to that magical moment. The next pages tell his story.

9

The One Thing

Like all things that are alive, the Vision Walk continues to grow and evolve. For years, I have used it in my workshops as a tool to create a stronger connection to the true self and a deeper communion with life. When I first explain the Vision Walk to my students, I suggest they start with the question, "What am I, and why am I here?"

The answers are always the same and always different. The authentic self listens and responds: "You are love, you are light, you are an angel, you are a meadow of wildflowers, you are a divine expression of the one life, you are everything." But for me to say it doesn't begin to do it justice. So let me give you one man's experience of this universal answer, an answer that I hope will tempt you to ask the same question yourself.

At the Springbrooke Retreat Centre in Langley, British Columbia, I led a small group of Vision Walkers through the usual meditation, then sent them out to find their answers to the question, "What am I, and why am I here?" Among the walkers was my friend Bob Talbot. Bob is generally a quiet, practical man, a businessman with a powerful spirit tempered by a healthy dose of skepticism. When we had all assembled again after the walk, the participants recounted their experiences, one by one. Bob went last. He spoke slowly, thoughtfully:

"As I walked outside, I thought I was going to go down to the river, but I didn't. Instead, I was drawn to the far end of the field. There is a swampy pond over there and a number of big fir trees. I chose a tree and sat down.

"As I was sitting there listening to all the sounds of the birds, a strange thing happened. I noticed that I could actually hear the water moving in the ground beneath my feet. There were people, too. I could hear voices in the next block and the sound of cars in the distance. I closed my eyes and listened more attentively, taking it all in.

"Suddenly it came to me that this was a concert. It was all a beautiful, integrated, unified composition. As one sound would rise, another would fall and go under. I just sat there and listened to this beautiful music of the universe."

At this point, Bob became quiet and looked around as if wondering whether to continue. Then he said, "It was a gift to myself, actually, to feel and experience the unity of life. And as I sat there, I . . . I . . ." his voice choked with emotion: ". . . I became a tree."

We all felt the truth of what he was saying. His words, punctuated by quiet sobs, were all the proof we needed.

"My feet became roots growing into the earth," he continued. "My arms became branches reaching into the sky. Then I spread out even more. I was no longer in my body, but I felt it as a part of me. I was all of it— I became the wind, the earth, the sky, the voices, the birdsong, the people, the cars, the whole symphony. I was completely unified with everything. You guys," he said passionately, "there is only one thing!"

Bob brushed his face with his sleeve and regained his composure while the rest of us felt the impact of what he had said.

"When I finally opened my eyes, I realized that this life is a huge distraction. As I looked around, all the different forms were so beautiful, so filled with light. But then I started to lose that feeling of integration. Suddenly I realized that what I was now seeing was the illusion. It had captured my focus and pointed it away from the unity of all things. As I focused on the park and the ducks in the pond, I started to lose the car sounds and the people. I got drawn in and focused into a very narrow experience instead of a more expansive one. I realized at that point that the challenge is to be sensitive to the community of everything instead of the distractions."

As he spoke, we heard the wailing sound of a train whistle in the distance. "I realize now that the sound of that train is as much a part of the now moment as that fir tree outside the window, and just as beautiful. It's all vibrational, all harmonious, all integrated. That's my heart's desire," he said softly, "to know that all the time."

A mystic might say that Bob had experienced *satori*, the ecstatic experience of becoming one with all things. Whatever we call it, he experienced the truth, and that truth is available to all of us. The fact is, we already *are* one with all things, whether we experience it or not. As Bob said, we don't usually feel it because we distract ourselves. We distract ourselves with anything having to do with our separate selves. In a nutshell, we distract ourselves with our own thinking, which is almost always focused on the past and the future, hardly ever on the one moment we ever have: right here and now.

We can all get back to that moment of oneness, that

experience of being the one thing. We can all re-attune ourselves to the music of that universal symphony, just by slowing down and letting go. Almost anything can help take us back to our true self—a Vision Walk, a quiet moment in a meadow, a deep breath in a traffic jam, a warm smile, a cheerful thought. It's all a choice, and it's all so simple.

10

The Real You Meditation

I want to offer you one more tool for mastery: a deeper experience of the real you. As with the Vision Walk Meditation, for best results, I suggest you record this meditation and play it back while you are listening quietly, or have someone read it to you calmly and slowly. While you are recording or reading the meditation, be sure to pause for a moment when you see dots like this: . . .

Begin by sitting comfortably in a chair or on the floor. Close your eyes and breathe slowly and gently. . . . Just let down and relax completely. . . . Feel your breath coming and going. . . . Now notice what you feel inside your body. Notice any areas of comfort or discomfort, pain or pleasure. Also notice any thoughts or feelings that arise. . . . This is the "you" you think you are—your body, mind, and emotions.

Now imagine that there is another you standing about 10 feet behind your body. Imagine it is an exact replica of your physical body, wearing the exact same clothes. Notice, however, that this body has no thoughts, no feelings. This is your dream body. Notice the difference between your dream body and your physical body. . . .

Now look at your physical body through the eyes of your dream body. Notice the details—the hair, the back of the head, the way the body is sitting, the slow rhythmical breath moving in and out of the lungs. When you can see your physical body clearly through the eyes of your dream body, walk around your physical body and notice it from different angles—from the back, the side, the front, and the other side. Take your time as you do this. . . .

Now allow your dream body to fade and disappear, but continue watching your physical body. Notice that you no longer have a dream body—you are pure awareness—but you can still see your physical body.

Imagine your awareness slowly circling your physical body, just as you did before. . . . Now imagine that you are looking at your physical body from somewhere up near the ceiling. Notice the appearance of the top of the head, the shoulders, the clothes, the arms and legs. Notice how different they look from this angle.

Now, as pure awareness, allow your focus to spread out. Become the space surrounding your physical body. Imagine *you are gently holding your physical body, cradling it in nothingness, providing the space for it to be. Let yourself be the consciousness that surrounds your body.*

Now spread out and become the empty space surrounding your home. . . . When you are ready, expand to surround your entire neighborhood. . . . Now expand to encompass your entire city. . . . When you are ready, feel what it is like to surround the entire planet with your awareness. Finally, allow your attention to drift past the moon and into outer space. . . . Expand even more and allow yourself to become the space between the stars.

Now, as empty space, feel yourself transmitting impulses of light and life across the universe—galaxy to living galaxy, star to living star. Feel the stars radiating and pulsating within you. Feel what it's like to love them and hold them in place. Then feel what it's like to give birth to new stars and galaxies. . . .

Next, with a leap of the imagination, slowly allow yourself to return to your physical body. Let yourself seep into the space between the molecules and atoms of your body. Notice the vastness of inner space. Notice how being inner space compares with being outer space. . . . Finally, when you are ready, return to your "normal" state of consciousness.

Has your perspective changed? Who or what are you now?

Of course, who or what you appear to be is going

to change with your changing point of view. That's the whole point of the Real You Meditation. There is no "right" or "wrong" perspective; everything you perceive and how you perceive it—in fact, everything *everyone* perceives—is "right" from their point of view. So there's never anyone to blame or judge. The trick is to be able to shift and expand your point of view at will—to enjoy interacting in the world as a human being with a body, name, and personal history; then in the next moment shift your point of view to that of another very different person or object; and in the next moment remember that you are also the universe of pure awareness that embraces and embodies all forms.

Conclusion

It's Your Choice

Before I leave you to your practice, I want to say a few more things about choice. In a way, choice is what the Vision Walk is all about. Until we find the truth in our hearts, we really don't have much choice. We're mostly at the whim of our beliefs and programming. We're acting on automatic. The Vision Walk starts to make real choice possible by helping you change your point of view.

From the point of view of the conditioned mind, the world is a very scary place—a place where you need to protect and defend yourself from danger and death. The choices you make from that fear-based perspective will probably be very limited and constricting. From the perspective of the heart, which knows you are eternal and connected to all things, your choices—based in love—will tend to be much more expansive.

By now you know from firsthand experience that you can see new ways of looking at life by going to the source of who you really are. But what lies beyond this life? Is it possible to change your deep-seated beliefs and fears about death? The truth of that, too, is inside you. When you see it, it can change your perspective forever, not to mention your day-to-day choices about life.

In 1998 I had a near-death experience. (No, I hasten to say, it was not the result of a Vision Walk.) The circumstances don't matter much now, except to say that my heart was beating about 220. Other than that, I was lying peacefully under a tree, looking up at the stars and the moon through a canopy of leaves. Miguel, who fortunately is also a medical doctor, was kneeling by my side. He had already listened to my heart and quickly decided what needed to be done.

"Close your eyes and take a deep breath," he said.

I closed my eyes and took a deep breath. As I lay quietly beneath the tree seeing nothing but darkness, Miguel pushed his thumbs against my eyeballs. In that moment, the quality of my experience changed. I found myself floating freely in the blackness of empty space. In the far distance was a tiny star—a pinprick of light that grew quickly larger and brighter. As the light approached, it exploded with life, radiating sparks brighter than the blaze from an acetylene torch.

Just as I was marveling that it was possible to look directly at the sparks without going blind, they engulfed me, and I went blasting through a tunnel of light. The entire tunnel was composed of magnificent little sparks, each one sentient, intelligent, alive. Speeding past me in the opposite direction like stars in hyperspace, each one knew and loved me intimately, and I knew and loved them back. Somehow I knew they were rushing out from the void to have experiences in the world—to become trees, rocks, people, mosquitoes, whales, wildflowers—and I was rushing back to merge with the source of all things.

I was in utter ecstasy. "Oh, my God, Miguel!" I exclaimed. "Is this where you go?" Curiously, my talking to Miguel seemed perfectly normal. As normal as switching channels on a TV set. One moment I was tuned to Channel 7, looking up at the moon through the tree branches, the next I was on Channel 13, rushing through hyperspace in the *Starship Enterprise*.

Miguel's response to my question was blunt and matter-of-fact: "Now you know what it is like to die."

No, it can't be! I thought. *I've never felt more alive!* Like a drop of water that suddenly remembers it is part of the sea, all I wanted to do was rush down that pulsating river and merge with the unfathomable ocean of love at the other end.

Miguel did not buy my enthusiasm. "I'm talking with the archangels," he said firmly, "and they're telling me that if you go, you're not coming back! Take another breath."

As I took another breath, Miguel pushed back on my eyeballs again, and I went racing even further into the tunnel. I pleaded with him to come with me, insisting that we could travel all the way to the Source and come back to tell about it.

"If you don't listen to me, you're gonna be a goner," he warned.

Four times Miguel pushed back on my eyeballs, and four times I sped further through the tunnel, as oblivious to danger as a stone plummeting to the earth from a 40-story building. The gravitational pull of love was too powerful to resist.

Finally Miguel interrupted my near-fatal reverie with a quick whack of his fist on my chest. I returned involuntarily, and half an hour later I was lying on a comfortable bed chatting with Miguel about the experience.

"That was pretty amazing," I said, "but the most amazing thing was how powerful the pull was. I know you go through that tunnel all the time. *How do you ever get back?*"

Miguel smiled. "I love to visit God," he said.

"Each time I visit, I ask him, 'Can I stay with you this time?' And he says, 'Mmm, not yet. I have some more messages for you to deliver. After you deliver them, you come back again and we'll see.'"

"You mean you're like some kind of cosmic mailman?" I asked.

"You could put it that way," Miguel said. "Now get some sleep."

After a good night's sleep, I was hardly the worse for wear. But after my journey I was never the same, and neither was my world. My perspective had changed dramatically. Colors were brighter. Faces were more radiant. Life was more miraculous and inviting. The invisible world had become visible, palpable, almost tangible. The joy of consciousness emanated from everything—even from chairs, rocks, and refrigerators.

For weeks afterward, my heart felt like a glowing coal. I watched birds tumbling in the trees and felt their heartbeats as my own. I gazed into people's faces and saw myself as in a magic mirror. I listened to music and heard playful sparks of light singing messages of love and communion.

For months I tried to make sense of my experience. Years later, it is still a great mystery, but repeatedly it tells me this: *The tunnel of light is not out there; it's inside. God is in every cell, and every cell rejoices at the memory of its maker. We all came from the light, and we're all going back to it. In fact, we never left it. It's as present as the air we breathe.*

If that is true, then why not live it? Why not *be* the light? The answer to that question is in our beliefs and choices.

Back in Santa Fe a few weeks after my encounter with death (a word that to me seems laughable because even the most brilliant radiance of this life pales in comparison), Miguel asked me to recount my experience to the rest of his apprentices. I rambled on for over an hour. When I was done, Miguel added some comments of his own. I would like to include some of them here because they are so inspiring and so pertinent to the ultimate purpose of the Vision Walk and this book: to help you discover and experience the real you, to help you make wiser and more courageous choices, to help you live with joy instead of fear.

With that, I invite you to join Miguel's circle of apprentices. Just imagine that you are seated in the spacious, light-filled living room of a beautiful ranch house near Santa Fe, New Mexico, glimpsing through the window the fantastic rock formations that give this place the name, "The Garden of the Goddess." Imagine, as you read Miguel's words, that you can hear the rhythmic cadence of his voice and feel the truthful, loving energy of his heart. Imagine he is speaking directly to you.

Here is what he said:

I wanted Brandt to share his experience for one reason: for you guys to know the truth about what is in that place we call the "other side." It is something that is so obvious, but with all our intelligence we try to explain and justify. We complicate everything.

The truth is that there is only one living being in the entire universe, only one living being. The name is not important, but we call it God. There is only one. It is in everything, and it's obvious. We don't need to search for God. There is nothing to search for. We don't need for someone to take us to God, because everything you can perceive, sooner or later, is going back to God. More than that, everything is already with God. It's obvious: Everything and everybody is going back to God—even if you don't want to.

And if you don't need to work so hard looking for God, what is left for you? Isn't it obvious what is left? To be alive. To be happy. To do the best you can to enjoy the journey.

You can enjoy your life, or you can be miserable; it's your choice. You can beat yourself up and be abusive with yourself. You can create all those dramas around you. Or you can enjoy life. You can be nice—sharing, giving, receiving. Or you can be selfish and make everybody hate you. You can hurt people and get hurt. All that is just choices. Either way, you're going back to God.

Nobody is condemned. What you do during the journey is up to you. You can create your own hell right here. But it is your creation; it's you. And it all depends on what you believe. Whatever you believe is not true anyway. You can believe the worst about yourself, or you can believe the best about yourself. Either way, it's not the truth. It's just a dream. It's just a world of illusion. It's just a program that is put in the computer of your mind.

What is true is that you can choose how to play. You can choose to believe that you are the worst, or you can choose to believe that you are the best. Neither is true, but what do you enjoy? You can choose to play, or you can choose to be always serious. You can choose to judge everybody and make everybody wrong so you can be right. Or you can just relax and let the world be what it is. You can try to be in charge, to be responsible for everybody around you and suffer because they are not responsible. Or you can choose just to allow them to be, to love them the way they are, and have the best in every relationship you have.

You can choose to have all those resentments against your father, your mother, your brothers, your sisters. You can choose to be in conflict with them. You can choose to feel victimized for the way they guided you. You can choose to judge them and find them guilty and try to punish them. You can choose to play God, or you can choose just to love them, to forgive, to enjoy them before they die—or before you die. It's just choices.

You can choose to have a conflict with your partner in life. You can choose to make his or her life miserable and make yours miserable, too. You can choose to be so controlling that you create a nightmare in every relationship you have. Or you can choose to enjoy it, to be free, to love, to give, to share, to receive.

You can choose to live your life being afraid of every step you take. You can choose to create all those demons around you with your fears and be afraid to be what you are. Or you can choose to ignore them, not believe in them, to create all those angels who take care of you and enjoy them. It is your choice.

You can see that you are trapped in your own beliefs. You believe something is wrong. You believe something is not possible. You believe that you don't have the courage. Then, thy will be done. But it's your belief. If you believe that you're victimized, then you are victimized. If you believe that you cannot be happy, then you cannot be happy. It's about what you believe.

But if you know that your beliefs are not true, and that all those lies were ruling your life for all those years, perhaps you can be free of your own beliefs. You don't have to believe yourself anymore when you tell yourself that you're not good enough, not strong enough, not beautiful enough. You don't have to believe yourself when you tell yourself that you cannot make it. You don't have to believe yourself when you believe that nobody understands you and nobody loves you. You don't have to believe yourself when you believe that nobody cares about you, that everybody hates you. You don't have to believe any of that. It's just a concept, just a point of view.

To believe that you can be happy, to believe that you can love, to believe that you deserve love, joy, happiness, everything—it's just choices. Either way it's a world of illusion, the world of the human mind. Everything has meaning only because all of us agree. We agree on the meaning of every word in the language we use. We agree on all those concepts that rule society. We agree how things should be. But we invented it, we created it. All those concepts, all those beliefs, all those rules. We did it. Who says it's real? No, it is not real; it is not the truth.

What is not true <u>needs</u> to be believed. What is true doesn't need to be believed. It is what it is. And that is the power of the vision that Brandt had when he was dying. He saw what it is with no explanation.

Believe it or not, your body is made of atoms. You don't need to believe it, but it's made by atoms. Believe it or not, the sun is right there. You don't have to believe it; it is what it is. But for you to say, "I'm not worthy," you need to believe it. You have to believe it in order for it to become real. If you don't believe it, it means nothing; it's just a concept. It's a lie.

Lies need to be believed by you in order to exist. All your limitations need to be believed in order to be real. If you don't believe them, there are no limitations. They are gone, just like snapping your fingers. Then everything becomes just a choice. And that choice is true power.

Miguel always talks about beliefs and choices. And with good reason: Beliefs and choices are what determine our thoughts, feelings, actions, and destinies. What are your beliefs, and what are your choices?

From my point of view, the most powerful choices we can make are to find the truth of who we are and live our greatest dreams. The Creator is speaking to us all the time. We all have access to the word of God, every moment, right in the recesses of our own hearts. That is the central message of all great sages and spiritual paths. For followers of different religions to argue about which one is right or wrong is like two branches of the same tree arguing about which one is attached to the trunk. Beyond words, beyond books, beyond our wildest imaginings, the simple truth is staring us in the face every moment: *You are one with all that is, and you are here to enjoy this life.*

So let me conclude with a simple suggestion: Trust your own inner voice. By whatever means your spirit directs you, find your own truth, your own light, and let it shine. Discover your dream and live it, with no excuses. Take stock of your beliefs. Keep the ones that work, and throw the others in the trash. Make choices that will benefit yourself and everyone around you. Travel in good company, sharing your life and your dream with the ones you love. Along the way, stay as present as you can. And don't regret or worry about a thing. The only moment that matters is now. And if you still can't bring yourself to believe it, maybe it's time to take a walk. . . .

Appendices

Appendix A

Suggestions for Questions
(What do I ask in my Vision Walk?)

The questions you ask can determine the quality of your life. But sometimes it's difficult to know what to ask. To stimulate your mind, following are a few pages of questions listed by category. Even if these don't work for you, they may spark others you want to ask. These are only examples. Ask the questions that are important for *you*.

Spiritual and Life Questions

Who am I, and why am I here?

What is my life's purpose?

How can I realize my greatest dreams?

Which path is right for me?

What is the next step on my spiritual path?

What is my relationship to the divine?

What would my ideal life be like?

Where will I find true happiness?

What gifts do I have to give the world?

How can I feel more alive?

How can I get closer to spirit?

If I could have anything, what would it be?

What will bring me inner peace?

Who would be a good spiritual mentor?

How can I deepen my faith?

What would I do if I had six months to live?

Health Questions

How can I develop radiant health?

How can I stop smoking?

Why am I always so tired?

What is the ideal diet for me?

Why do the kids keep getting sick?

What foods or liquids should I avoid?

What's the best exercise program for me?

How can I reduce stress in my life?

What's the cure for this insomnia?

How can I wake up feeling refreshed?

Who can help me heal myself?

How does my thinking affect my health?

When am I going to get well?

Emotional Questions

How can I let go of fear?

What is the source of this fear?

What is the cause of my suffering?

How can I create more joy in my life?

When and how can I forgive?

Why do I feel so angry?

How can I express my gratitude?

How can I love unconditionally?

Why am I holding onto guilt and regret?

How will I feel when I let go of this?

Who is responsible for the way I feel?

Why do I take life so seriously?

How can I clear out the past?

Why am I avoiding this situation?

What is the solution to this situation?

Why does this pattern keep repeating itself?

What is the blessing in this problem?

How can I make the most of this experience?

Relationship Questions

What do I really want in a relationship?

Where can I find a mate?

How can I get her to notice me?

Why hasn't he called?

Why don't I call him?

Why does jealousy keep coming up?

What do I need to let go of in order to love?

How will I get through this heartbreak?

How can I ever love again?

How can we improve our communication?

What would put a new spark in our relationship?

How can we schedule more time together?

How can I show her how much I love her?

Which relatives shall we spend the holidays with?

How can we make this love last a lifetime?

Work and Career Questions

What is my ideal work or career?

What kind of people do I want to work with?

How can I double my income in two years?

What is the next step in my career?

When shall I give notice?

What goals will really motivate me?

What is the best use of my time?

How can I become more productive?

Is there anything we haven't considered?

What can I learn from this mistake?

Why does my boss keep passing me by?

What does my business need right now?

How can I attract more clients?

When do we need to have this completed?

What are my customers looking for?

How can I be of greater service?

Where do I want to be 10 years from now?

What is the solution to this problem?

What would I risk if I knew I couldn't fail?

Family Questions

What does family mean to me?

What are my family priorities?

How can I get along better with my kids?

What legacy do I want to leave my family?

Why am I avoiding my family?

How can I get everything done?

What values do I want to pass on to my kids?

How can I balance work and family?

When will we start the kids' education fund?

How can we get Jimmy to come out of his shell?

Who is responsible for this?

How can I regain my parents' trust?

How can we help the kids improve their grades?

What's the best kind of care for Grandpa?

Financial Questions

What are my financial priorities?

How can I make and save more money?

How much money do I really want?

Why don't I pay my bills on time?

How can I achieve financial independence?

Where shall I invest my money?

Will this investment pay off?

What is the solution to this financial problem?

How do my finances reflect my beliefs?

Will the economy be stronger or weaker next year?

What's the trend in the stock market?

How can I best plan for my kids' education?

When are we going to retire?

Everyday Questions

What's a good gift for my mother's birthday?

How I can I liven up my looks?

Who would be a good role model for me?

How can I have more fun?

What is the best holiday destination?

Where can I find what I'm looking for?

How can I resolve this problem?

Which of all these options is best for me?

Why do I find these people so difficult?

What is the best response to this situation?

Where do we go from here?

Who can give me the best advice?

Appendix B

Letters from Vision Walkers

Finally, I want to share parts of some letters I have received from Vision Walkers. Many of these were sent by friends in Vancouver, British Columbia, after a day-long workshop titled "Manifesting Your Dream" at the University of British Columbia First Nations Longhouse, a magnificent cedar structure with modern carvings and totem poles modeled after the Northwest native community centers of old. I include the letters here to give you a better feel for how the Vision Walk works, how specific and personal each one is, how the walks are interpreted, and how life changing they can be.

Letter #1

The first is from my friend Randy Bennett, who with his wife Joan organized the workshop for me. Initially Randy thought he hadn't gotten an answer.

I thought I should tell you that I now realize that my Vision Walk was actually answered. And within five minutes! My question was, "How will I achieve financial security?"

When I left the long house, I saw a large, wooden, square-shaped object directly across the street. I was being told my answer was there. I walked directly to it and realized it used to be covered with flyers but they had all been cleaned off. However, there were still some bits of paper stuck under the staples, and I looked for some words that might give me an answer. There was nothing that made sense, so I moved on. Then I saw some crows, and I also felt there was an answer there, but I couldn't understand what it might be.

So today I was telling Joan about my walk, and she said, "Duh! The big wooden square is advertising, Randy!" Duh, indeed! How did I miss that? And it was empty except for a few remnants, just like my business right now. But it can also mean that it's a clean slate ready to start again, with all new advertising and clients. I've been trying to hang on to my old clients when I need to go out and get new ones. The crows show me that. They are form shifters and represent transformation. By working through Spirit, they bring both the past and the future into the Now.

It was all there, but I must have come out of my heart and into my mind looking for the answer. A point I'll be sure to remember next time. This is truly amazing stuff!

Randy Bennett
Vancouver, British Columbia

Randy's story is quite magical, but even more magical is what happened after the workshop. Less than two weeks after his Vision Walk, Randy landed a huge advertising contract with a major land developer. He and an associate teamed up to bid alongside three of the best-known graphic and design firms in the city. Coincidence? Not at all. The power of the Vision Walk is that it aligns you with the real you, the you that has no doubt, that revels in taking risks, that knows exactly what you need to do and knows that you can do it.

Letter #2

The next letter is from an artist who was feeling frustrated over being "in limbo" for a long time.

My question was: "What is my next step with my art?"

I walked out into the sunshine and was drawn to a grove of tall cedar trees. I picked up an oval-shaped stone on the way, to help connect more deeply with the earth as I walked. As I stood in the center of the circle of trees, I felt comforted and at home.

Then I felt like walking out into the sunshine along a walkway. I came upon a tall metal gate that was chained and padlocked. I walked up to the gate and looked into the courtyard beyond. It struck me that the gate represented my self-imposed limitations, so I stood in front of it and imagined having the key to unlock it.

I saw myself unlocking it so the heavy metal chain fell away. Then I imagined entering the courtyard, which symbolized my Inner Courtyard where all the answers were to be found. Then something told me to turn around and look down—and there on the ground at my feet was a bottle cap that read: HAPPY PLANET.

I gasped, "Oh My God!" because there was my answer. That is the purpose of my art, to do my part to help create a happy planet!

It all seemed so clear now. I want my grandchildren to grow up on a happy planet. So now my art has a much higher purpose.

Annette Shaw
Galiano Island, British Columbia

There are several things I want to point out about this Vision Walk. First, notice how Annette's intuition told her to pick up a stone to represent the earth. Through a simple act of faith, the stone became a power object for her—an object that bypassed her mind and aligned her with her deeper intent.

She also took the Vision Walk a step further. She not only received an answer, but in her profound state of alignment she actually *changed her inner reality.* She began consciously interacting with the elements of her waking dream. She decided to imagine having the key to unlock her gate of self-imposed limitations. She did this in such a deep state of faith that it actually happened. Having done that, she was able to enter her own Inner Courtyard, and it was there that she found the bottle cap.

On one level, what happens in the Vision Walk is symbolic and mythological. Yet it is exactly at the level of myth—the level of the deep subconscious—that profound and lasting change happens. It is here and only here that old beliefs are shattered and new ones come into being. Remember: Everything is a mirror. Change your inner world, and the outer world changes to reflect it.

Letter #3

Here is a letter that revolves around an especially compelling question.

I asked, "How can I focus in one direction in order to find my joy and passion?"

I wandered into the sunlight and started meandering around the wonderful UBC campus. I felt an affinity with the budding of the trees and the spring flower blossoms, but as I walked past a wrought-iron fence I looked into the interior of a grove of fir trees and saw something that really arrested my vision. It looked like a baby stroller perched on top of an ancient tree stump! From the look of the logger's notches, the tree must have been logged in the 1920s.

I had to circle a large building to enter the little grove. When I did, I realized I could climb up and perch on another stump about nine feet up. This second stump was a nurse log for a struggling young huckleberry bush, one of my favorite plants in the woods.

I found myself repelled by the stroller as an object, as it was clearly so much a part of the "manufactured" world. It marred the whole experience of enjoying the grove. As I sat and contemplated the situation, I realized that what I was witnessing was the contrast between two things that were totally incongruous and inappropriate, compared to the beautiful nurse log I was balancing on.

The "Aha!" came when I realized that I have been wishing to be someone other than who I am. Wanting to apply what works for others to my own life and my own dream. How ridiculous and unproductive! And basically how ugly the result of that can be, when I am ignoring the beauty of the life I have created for myself using the tools and tendencies and struggles of my own unique approach to life.

The symbols struck me as a sort of reprimand for not accepting my true self and therefore not practicing gratitude for my own great vision. It reinforced the understanding that I need to move on my path using my own gait, pace, and style, staying focused on the experience of every moment, and trust that the process will indeed take me where I need to go.

Lianne Smithaniuk
British Columbia, Canada

There were many powerful symbols in Lianne's Vision Walk. But it's important to remember that someone else might have interpreted them very differently. Someone else may have felt uneasy in the grove and found the stroller reassuring, or perhaps symbolic of nurturing or new life. Remember, only you can say what the symbols mean for you. And you do this by checking in on your feelings.

Letter #4

This letter goes right to the heart of things:

My question was, "What is my heart's desire?" Throughout the five-minute meditation, I repeated the question over and over, not really knowing how to feel it. Meditation ended, my question left in a balloon out to the universe. I left the long house immediately and felt pushed in one direction. I stopped and noticed a bird perched on one of the buildings. I was aware of the wind song, the sunshine, the trees, the stillness. I watched a squirrel freely moving about. Then I realized, My God, that's it! That's my hearts desire! To be free!

Tears streamed down my face as I continued to walk. Then I noticed a sign that said "Faculty/Staff."

"Is that significant?" I asked myself? I put my hand to my heart, and I felt that it was. Then came the realization, My heart's desire is to teach freedom! The tears continued. I thought of the many times I had muttered the words, "I just wish I was free." So, I asked myself, "What makes the word freedom so significant now? Because it didn't come from my head! came the answer. I was completely dumbfounded. I really felt brand new in that moment!

Next I noticed a sign that read, "This area has been sprayed for weed control."

"Is that significant?" I asked again? Yes, it is, my inner

voice said. Watch what you focus on. The weeds are your "Don't Wants" that keep you from manifesting your heart's desire.

Throughout my journey of almost 40 years, I have experienced a great deal of pain and suffering. In fact, at some level I have become so attached to being the victim that I have forgotten what it is like to be free. I have been aware of this for years now. But without action, awareness changes nothing. It's the car without the key. I have self-helped myself to near-death over the years, searching for the something that would give me the key. Now I have it.

Cheryl Dickson
Langley, British Columbia

Notice how Cheryl's Vision Walk answered more than one question. Like her, you may find that once you are in the proper state of mind, you begin to have not just a Vision Walk, but a Vision *Talk* or Vision *Conversation* with your environment. This is you talking to you. This is the ocean talking to the drop. This is you getting answers, fresh meaning, and direction from your own reflection in the things around you.

Letter #5

The next two letters are also good examples of extending the Vision Walk into a Vision Talk or Vision Conversation.

I have spent many years feeling that no matter how much or what I do is not good enough. My question for my Vision Walk was, "What is my life calling?" My hope was to receive confirmation on my calling and send out my intentions to lead me where I need to be in order to develop myself.

My first awareness on my walk was a large sign that read NO ADMITTANCE WITHOUT PERMISSION!

At the entrance to the Nitobe Memorial Gardens, I thought I must go in there. There was a ticket booth, but I had no money with me. I stood and listened to someone else from the workshop trying to enter and heard the lady in the booth say, "I can't say yes to that!"

I began to walk away, thinking, "Right, no admittance without permission. My life's story, waiting for someone to recognize me and give me permission to go ahead.

I turned back around to see the other woman enter. With that, I thought, "What could I give the woman in the ticket booth so that I might enter?"

Then it came to me: Give her your word. Give her your word that you will return at lunchtime with the admittance fee. A moment later, having done this, I entered the magical gardens in total awe and gratitude.

Inside the gardens there was a long row of lanterns. The first lantern that gave me a message was the Change of Life Lantern. My second message came from the Remembering Lantern. My final messages were from the Stepping Stones Lantern and the Heaven on Earth Lantern.

Once I returned to the long house and sat down, I sent out a prayer of gratitude to the Creator for the gifts I had received. At lunchtime, I not only returned to honor my word, I also brought my husband and another student back to the Magical Gardens and paid their way. We enjoyed a wonderful potluck lunch together and sharing time. We then revisited our Vision Walks.

Wendy Kropf
British Columbia, Canada

In this next Vision Walk, notice the many images that "speak," the ongoing conversation with the deeper self, and the internal changes that occur spontaneously during the walk.

Letter #6

My question was, "Why was my son taken from me, and how can I use this experience of death and grieving to help others?

After the meditation, I got up from my seat and walked toward the sunlight and into the outdoors. The smell of spring was in the air, and a slight breeze gently guided me toward a nearby building. I was drawn to the stairs.

As I began ascending the stairs, slowly, one by one, I felt heat and warmth from the sun, its light surrounding me. It was then that I affirmed that my son's death had given me the opportunity to grow spiritually. Each step became another level of awareness, a step closer on the journey to enlightenment.

The wooden stairs were covered with a screen-like mesh, and I could see that I had had a screen covering this part of my life that was once so important to me. It was hard to see through this screen, but now it was off, and I knew it was time to let the light in. I breathed deeply and walked slowly down the stairs, ready to look for signs to assist me in answering the next part of my question.

I began walking on the sidewalk leading from the stairs. It was cracked and worn. Bits of tree roots and moss and fungus were oozing from the cracks. They looked like gaping wounds that needed to be closed. They reminded me of the wounds from the death of a child that are so terribly difficult to heal. They were everywhere I looked. Seeing them, I realized that so many mothers and fathers like myself shared in this pain and needed healing, too.

I saw myself supporting these people, helping them to get through their time of grieving, shining love and understanding on them, helping them to heal their horrible wounds. I knew then that this was the service I needed to do.

Next, I moved across the green grass and was drawn toward the corner of another building. The trail that led along the edge of this building ended abruptly in a corner. I felt trapped and isolated, alone. This is how many people feel after the death of a child, I am sure—trapped in their pain and grief, isolated and alone with their feelings. This only reinforced the fact that I needed to reach out to them.

Walking out into the open and looking around, I was impressed by the beauty of the cherry blossoms floating down to the ground, their subtle, pink blossoms lying on the rich green of the grass. I looked around again and saw plants and trees in many stages of growth, some dormant, some bursting with new life. In that instant, I saw the cycle of life, of growth and death, of change. I was struck by the *reality of life as a cycle of birth and death, a cycle that we all experience. Some of us have a longer time and some a shorter time, just as the many plants and trees surrounding me. It is a natural cycle. It is shortened for some, but life continues. I felt as if I needed to carry on with my life, work toward restoring joy in it, helping others, and continue on the spiritual path that has been renewed, recognizing that I will once again be reunited with my son.*

As I returned to the place where my Vision Walk began, I heard the sound of a waterfall nearby. To me, it symbolized the flow of life, and it brought a feeling of peace.

Terry Milos
Pender Harbour, British Columbia

By now I hope you're getting a feel for how personal each Vision Walk is, as well as a better idea of how to interpret them. I am including a few more letters that show the inspiring insights possible in a Vision Walk.

Letter #7

My question started as a basic, "Will I be happy?" followed by "Where will I find my happiness?" and lastly, "What will truly make me happy?"

I approached the walk with my usual fear thoughts: What if I don't get it? What if I don't see anything?

I left the building and took off in one direction, only to feel drawn to another. When I passed a sign about an area being treated for weeds, I reflected on my family history of entanglement, enmeshment, and generally well-rooted dysfunction. But there was nothing really there.

Then I noticed a squirrel. Hmm, I thought. A bit like me, flitting about here and there. Intimate relationships have always been a challenge for me, and hoarding. Hoarding money for my retirement because I am afraid to be poor. Hoarding family stuff because it is history. Accumulating and hoarding stuff because it fills the empty part of the soul.

I was frustrated. Was I trying too hard to find the answer? I headed back to the long house. Once inside, I found myself ducking around corners, ending up in a room where photographs of prominent members of the native community were hung around the room.

As I surveyed the room, I burst into tears. At one end of the room hung a framed saying, "To honor one is to honor all." I was in the Honor Room, and there was my answer:

My true happiness will be found in honoring myself. When I can truly do this, then all other happiness will be available to me, because I will no longer be struggling with myself.

As I stood in the room, I thought, I wanted to see myself the way others have said they see me, and to truly believe what they have said.

When I left the room to rejoin the group, I found myself looking into a window that happened to be a mirror. There I was, reflected in the mirror. I was stunned, and I asked myself, Is this me? And this time it was. I was really seeing and honoring myself for the first time.

Along with honoring myself comes the feeling that over the years I have allowed myself to under-achieve, under-perform, and underestimate my own self-worth . . . the old family, weedy, suffocating stuff.

Judy Chrastina
Vancouver, British Columbia

Letter #8

My question was, "How can I give expression to my spiritual quest and being?

I was guided to the corner entrance to an old building across the lawn. I had a sense that I would see a sign—not a metaphor but an actual sign. When I reached the corner of the building, after passing many signs (none of which spoke to me), I saw a plaque on the wall. It commemorated a Mrs. Ross, after whom the building was named, and it listed her many contributions to the university. The sign drew me to it, but the words meant little, except to remind me of my grandmother.

I turned around to walk back from where I came, trying to block all thoughts that I must have gone the wrong way and would not receive an answer. I was near panic when I suddenly looked up. As my eyes feasted on the image before me, I gasped for breath, my tears fell, and my heart filled. I had received a vision with three symbols: a huge willow tree, one magnificent branch that spiraled up into the sky, and a raven sitting on one of the willow branches, its feathers gleaming in the sun.

I stood at the base of the willow and began to shake from head to toe. I immediately felt the presence of my grandmother. Grandma has been dead for six years now, and she had come to me a number of times before in meditations and psychic readings. One of my favorite places in the world was her house. One of the most magical places at Grandma's was under the willow tree that stood in the back of her yard—a place full of delicious, warm, summer garden scents.

The raven sat on a thick branch midway up the tree. His feathers gleamed silver in the sun. A raven was recently given to me by a young aboriginal woman who was volunteering in our school. The gift was an acknowledgment of my leadership in the school. The spiraling branch was on the other side of the tree, and it gave the appearance of spiraling up into heaven.

So my answer was this: "Your grandmother is your guide; she is with you always. The raven is your totem; study and learn from him. The spiral to heaven means stay on your spiritual path."

Anne Skelcher
British Columbia, Canada

Letter #9

My question was, "What attachments do I need to give up?"

The first thing of significance I saw was one of my favorite Renoir female nudes. (Obvious message there, I think!) The next was a half-finished bottle of whiskey. Then I found myself going around and around in circles of about six feet in diameter. After the first couple of circles, I stopped moving and tried to quieten my mind, but there was no doubt I was meant to be going around and around.

This continued for quite some time until I eventually felt that I needed to lie down. I did, only to find myself looking directly up at a light fixture—so directly, in fact, that I was struck by the perfect symmetry of the light from my perspective.

While the light is a mystery to me in view of my question, the image of me chasing my own tail around in circles, only to collapse in a heap, was quite vivid and, I think, very much applies to several areas of my life. But I'm also pleased that the real me should have such a funny way of expressing himself!

Chris Turner
Melbourne, Australia

This letter is a perfect example of how sometimes the things you *do* during your Vision Walk can become your best answers. And yes, the real you *does* have funny ways of expressing itself. Funny, outrageous, joyful, loving, unpredictable—the real you is endlessly creative! As for the vision of the light, I suspect that Chris has discovered by now that his true self was simply showing him the *result* of letting go of his attachments. When we cease running in circles, we finally see the light!

Letter #10

Through the years, many people have incorporated the Vision Walk into their lives as a kind of ongoing reality check. Tom is a good example:

The question I had on my first Vision Walk was, "What is my purpose in life?"

After I finished the meditation, I got up and walked around my living room. Nothing really responded to me. Then, as I walked into my office, my attention was drawn to a Newsweek magazine that was lying on the floor. The headline on the cover was, "How to Win the Peace?" However, all I saw were the words, "To Win the Peace." The letters stood out in a way I cannot even describe. They looked as if they were glowing and jumping out of the magazine in 3-D. I started laughing and crying at the same time. I was amazed at how fast I had gotten my answer. It didn't even take five minutes!

On my second Vision Walk, I asked the question, "How can I be of service to my family?" This question was very important to me, as there is great unhappiness within my family. I drove to the lake and listened to the Vision Walk meditation in my car. Then I sat on the beach for a while. A few minutes later, I got up again and walked around. At one point, I stopped walking, knowing that I had to look around right where I was. As I gazed in all directions, I noticed that

I was surrounded by about 15 to 20 trash cans. All of them had the words written on them, "Put the trash in its place."

I knew this was my answer, but I was confused. I wasn't quite sure what it meant, so I asked the question, "What does that mean?" I received the answer that it has to do with truth, that all I need to do is point to the truth. That was it. I could feel the answer in my entire body. Again, I was fascinated at how easily and directly I received the answer.

Finally, last weekend I planned to fly to California. I had a funny feeling about this trip from the moment I purchased the ticket. I decided to do a Vision Walk and ask if I should go or not. The answer came back in the form of a thought. I heard the words, "Do not decide now. Be very aware, and decide when you get to the airport."

When I arrived at the Chicago airport, I asked again, "Should I go on this trip?" The answer came lightning fast: "NO!" But I was not sure if this wasn't just my head talking, so I dismissed the thought and boarded the plane.

The plane left after an hour's delay and circled for another hour above Philadelphia due to heavy air traffic. When we finally landed, my connecting flight to San Francisco was gone. I took the next plane back to Chicago and was quite amused about how easily this could have been avoided if I had just listened.

Tom Gruner
Chicago, Illinois

I want to point out several things about Tom's Vision Walks. First, the words "glowing and jumping out of the magazine in 3-D." When you are in the Vision Walk frame of mind—that is, no-mind—you are actually perceiving in a different way. You are seeing through the same eyes, but without the filter of the mind. With the mind shut down, you are free to perceive through the heart. Thus, you are able to see more deeply, more richly, and in some ways more truly. The images you receive are still being projected onto the physical screen of the retina, but they are being *interpreted* through the heart.

This is a very active process. You might even call it an artistic creation. Consider the deep magic of it: Through your heart, the real you, which is infinitely more than your body or mind, is actually directing your body toward specific objects and experiences, which it then uses as symbols to communicate with you in its own unique language. It even magnifies, manipulates, and distorts certain images so that you will take notice and get the message more clearly. What could be more magical than that?

Equally magical, it is obvious from Tom's story about the plane flight that the real you has an amazing ability to "predict" what we call "the future." Unbounded by the illusions of time or space, your authentic self experiences everything as here and now, including events occurring in what most of us perceive as past and future. With such "wide-angle vision," it has access to an incomprehensibly enormous picture, and it can tell us the probable results of almost any action we take.

Whether we are willing to listen to its advice is another story. Most often we are not, simply because we are in the habit of listening to our minds instead of our hearts. With practice, however, we can all learn to trust the wisdom of the true self. Then heart and mind can work in harmony, the heart providing the wisdom and direction and the mind providing the thinking power to manifest our heart's desires.

Letter #11

This final Vision Walk account is from a woman who was attending a Toltec Easter celebration with don Miguel Ruiz in San Diego, during which I led a group Vision Walk.

I wanted to share with you about my Easter Vision Walk. My question was more of a plea: "Show me how to choose love over suffering."

I walked a bit and then went to my hotel room and sat. I just held my question and waited. I don't have a TV at home, so having one in the room was quite a treat. I was tempted to turn on the TV but felt that it would take me out of myself and the exercise. On the other hand, nothing was coming, so I figured, "Why not?"

I turned on the TV and was attracted to a movie. I watched a few minutes, and then something came. The characters were in prison. One was a musician. She was playing her new song for her friends. The words were, "We're building a dream, so break down the walls."

The words touched me deeply. I cried, then turned off the TV and sat some more. I then entered a hell so violent and painful it made me wretch. The Prince of Lies took possession of me, and I spiraled into the blackest black. I thought my heart light would be stamped out for good. I couldn't understand why this was happening. Why isn't

Spirit answering my question? I wondered.

Then it dawned on me. I began to see how I had lived my entire life from the experiences of others. I had betrayed myself again and again. I was livid. The tears were falling from my eyes as if the water was overflowing from a full glass.

At this point, my roommate entered. Seeing me crying, she came to me concerned. At her touch, I lost it. Something left me in a sort of primal heave. I felt dizzy, sick to my stomach, and ran to the bathroom.

When it was gone, it was gone. Afterwards, when I went back downstairs to the celebration, don Miguel was sitting alone onstage, and I instinctively went to him. For the first time in four years, I really allowed him to hold me. I received the exquisite and joyous gift of his love. I chose love over suffering! And my heart opened wide. Spirit had answered my question with a brilliant and unquestionable teaching: "JUST SAY YES!"

Beth
Albuquerque, New Mexico

Beth's experience is rare, but it does happen. In this case, her desire to overcome her own suffering was so strong that she demanded an answer. Ask and ye shall receive. Ask with a deep need, belief, and expectancy, and ye shall receive *immediately*. Her true self not only gave her an answer, it actually reached inside her and scooped out the negative programming of decades.

"We're building a dream, so break down the walls." These words, reflecting the truth of Beth's own internal prison, came as a command, and she carried it out. She broke down the walls. She left the past behind. She didn't think about it, she didn't analyze it, she just did it. This is intent at its best. It takes a lot of courage and magic to clear such powerful programs, but if you've really had enough suffering, it can happen. It can happen to anyone, and it can happen instantly.

Each of these letters reflected a unique and very personal experience. Each brought its Vision Walker new purpose, direction, and wisdom. It even changed many of their lives. It can do the same for you.

Appendix C

Vision Walk Journal

The following pages are offered to help you practice the Vision Walk and create a record of the messages you receive from the real you.

Here is how it works: First, write down the date and your question. Then, after your walk, reflect on your experience. Where did you go? What did you do? What did you see, hear, smell, taste or touch? Most important, what did you feel about these things?

Also, reflect on what things stood out like sore thumbs. What things especially drew your attention? These are your symbols. Write these down, too. Then, perhaps using some helpful hints from Chapter 6, Interpreting Your Walk, write down what the symbols mean to you. Finally, let your intuition put it all together and write down your answer. That's all there is to it.

Vision Walk Journal

Date:

Question:

Experience:

Symbols:

Meanings:

Answer:

Vision Walk Journal

Date:

Question:

Experience:

Symbols:

Meanings:

Answer:

Vision Walk Journal

Date:

Question:

Experience:

Symbols:

Meanings:

Answer:

Vision Walk Journal

Date:

Question:

Experience:

Symbols:

Meanings:

Answer:

Vision Walk Journal

Date:

Question:

Experience:

Symbols:

Meanings:

Answer:

Vision Walk Journal

Date:

Question:

Experience:

Symbols:

Meanings:

Answer:

Vision Walk Journal

Date:

Question:

Experience:

Symbols:

Meanings:

Answer:

Vision Walk Journal

Date:

Question:

Experience:

Symbols:

Meanings:

Answer:

Vision Walk Journal

Date:

Question:

Experience:

Symbols:

Meanings:

Answer:

Vision Walk Journal

Date:

Question:

Experience:

Symbols:

Meanings:

Answer:

Vision Walk Journal

Date:

Question:

Experience:

Symbols:

Meanings:

Answer:

ACKNOWLEDGMENTS

I would like to express my deepest gratitude to Tom Brown, Jr. for opening wide the doors of spirit during my first vision quest more than 20 years ago. In equal measure I would like to thank Miguel Ruiz for his unfathomable wisdom, enormous love, and unshakable faith. Thanks also to native peoples all over the world who love and respect the earth as a living being.

Cathy Dees, my editor at St. Lynn's Press, thank you for seeing so clearly just what this book needed in order to come alive. A big round of gratitude to Paul Kelly and the entire staff at St. Lynn's for the loving care that went into all aspects of the design and production. Thanks also to Janet Mills, Karen Kreiger, and the staff at Amber-Allen Publishing for reading and making extensive suggestions that strengthened the manuscript; to Lori Sherman for insightful and enthusiastic "anytime" editorial support; and to Larry Andrews (author of *Secrets of the Silk Road)* for leading me to St. Lynn's Press.

Jillianne Zimmerman, Caron Coke, Gloria Jean, Dick Kluckhohn, and Ruthie Donnellan, thanks for your friendship, compassion, and common sense, especially in trying times. Alex and Judy Shester and Brad Willis, thank you for guiding me through the storm. I would also like to thank Cathy Townsend, Cari Cole and Leslie Keehn for professional advice and encouragement; Carol Toone for holding intent; Dad and Mom for decades of love; Cheryl Dickson for vision; Joan and Randy Bennett, Jamie Gilroy, Meghan McChesney Gilroy, Laura Plumb, Larry and Carol Simpson, Lisa Longworth, Ron Wolf, Sandy Asch, Steve and Jen Romeo, Tatyana Curtis, Shari Naismith, Joanna Martinelli, Tom Gruner, and Paula Banfield for believing; Maud Sejournant and my French and Swiss friends for participating in the first Vision Walk near Santa Fe, New Mexico; and Sheri Rosenthal (author of *The Complete Idiot's Guide to Toltec Wisdom*) for "Results!"

I would also like to thank many personal friends and colleagues who have dedicated themselves to sharing their love for the earth, humanity, and all Creation. Among them are John Stokes of the Tracking Project; Malcolm Ringwalt of the Earth-Heart Institute of Vision and Healing; Frank and Karen Sherwood of Earthwalk Northwest; Jose Lucero of Santa Clara Pueblo; singer/songwriter James Nihan; Jamie Sams, author of *Medicine Cards*; John Freesoul, author of *Breath of the Invisible*; Bernadette Vigil, author of *The Mastery of Awareness*; Ray Dodd, author of *The Power of Belief* and *BeliefWorks*; Heather Ash, author of *The Four Elements of Change*; Susyn Reeve, author of *Choose Peace and Happiness* and *The Gift of the Acorn*; Susan Gregg, author of *The Toltec Way* and *The Complete Idiot's Guide to Spiritual Healing*; Allan Hardman, Barbara Emrys, Jose Luis Ruiz, Judy Ruiz, Gini Gentry, Rita Rivera, Ed Fox, Ted and Peggy Raess, Gary and Leo Van Warmerdam, Niki Oreitas, Aaron Landman, Rebecca Haywood, Gene Nathan, Oksana Yufa, Lee McCormick, Dennis and Lina Carruth, Hunter Flournoy, Fu Ding Cheng, Linda Jacobson, Mary Ann Granieri, Maggie Caffery, Susan Marshall, Hal Forman, Stephanie Bureau, Laura Paxton, Lennie Tan, Deidre Bainbridge, Jasmine Gold, Ron LaMee, Katherine Roxlo, Eve Bentley, Jeff and Vicky Warford, Tamara Messenger, and countless others in the ever-growing family of Toltec Teachers; my late friend and teacher Robert Boissiere and his wife Myla Vance; my brothers of the Banana Clan in Santa Fe; Rafael Quintanilla, Robert Eagle Hawk, and my sundancer friends at Taos Pueblo and San Cristobal, New Mexico; and numerous other friends from many Native American tribes. Thanks also to Jeffrey Ellis and

Rick "Two Hawks" Bennett, two departed brothers whose spirits continue to uplift and inspire.

Finally, thanks to all my students who have given me so much over so many years; to all those who provided written feedback after their first Vision Walks; to the members of the Coyote Thunder Medicine Society; and to my beautiful Toltec Dreamer family for their boundless love and inspiration.

About the Author

Brandt Morgan is a writer and teacher whose passion is helping people discover their true selves and realize their greatest dreams. He offers personalized coaching programs and conducts classes and workshops throughout the United States, Canada, and Europe. He also leads journeys to inspiring places such as Teotihuacan, Mexico, the birthplace of the Toltec tradition. He can be reached through his website at www.brandtmorgan.com.